A Chance to
LEARN

SAMUEL GILBERT

NEWMAN SPRINGS PUBLISHING
320 Broad Street
Red Bank, NJ 07701

First originally published by Newman Springs Publishing 2023

ISBN 979-8-88763-902-4 (Paperback)
ISBN 979-8-88763-903-1 (Digital)

Printed in the United States of America

INTRODUCTION

Greetings! It is truly remarkable that, after six decades, I find myself inspired and given the opportunity to delve into the historical and current struggles of Black Americans in the South and various states across the nation. Despite enduring immense hardships, such as poverty, their predicaments are seldom addressed by the media. Regrettably, I fear that without direct action from politicians who recognize the urgent need for change, these issues will persist, leaving them neglected. They are now hopeful that their struggles can be remedied before White supremacists' prejudiced attitudes towards Black individuals worsen.

I would deeply appreciate it if fellow Americans could spare a moment to peruse this book. I am confident that you will find the accounts of Black people's experiences in life-and-death circumstances intriguing and thought-provoking. So, fasten your seat belts and prepare for a challenging journey through the past, present, and future. While reading this book may be unsettling as you venture further into an era that few of us would have survived—enduring the unimaginable conditions of physical and mental enslavement by White supremacists—please know that it is entirely understandable.

CHAPTER 1

In the depths of the night, I awoke, my mind troubled by vivid dreams of my ancestors and the adversities they endured amidst harsh conditions. The thought of their suffering was deeply unsettling, as I imagined the torment of the unknown, their existence reduced to mere captives, treated no better than caged animals. The images that played in my dream felt all too real, evoking a sense of horror and leaving me with a lingering feeling of queasiness. Nevertheless, my resolve to delve deeper into their experiences persisted, eager to uncover their resilience despite being bound and lashed after arduous days toiling in the fields.

As I sought solace in sleep once again, a glimmer of hope arose within me, yearning to learn of their aspirations and dreams for future generations, their children and grandchildren. How did they envision a brighter tomorrow after enduring years of torture and death in their relentless pursuit of freedom? Alas, instead of ancestral revelations, I discovered a disheartening truth: politicians, driven by their own ambitions, employed whatever means they deemed necessary to construct this nation's prosperity, often at the expense of black lives, exploiting their labor and suppressing their potential. It was a profound revelation that shook me to the core, painting a grim picture of how this country was founded - off the record and on the weary backs of black individuals - all in the relentless pursuit of wealth and dominance over other nations.

Reflecting upon their immense suffering, I find myself grappling with the weight of this unresolved issue, contemplating who is now willing to empathize with the cruelties inflicted upon them, which have not yet been fully eradicated. Despite the passage of time and the end of that specific era of slavery, I remain hopeful that we can bridge the divide between us by embracing a more civilized approach. This presents an opportunity for us to exemplify the true meaning of fortitude through our actions, focusing on positive endeavors we can collectively achieve, devoid of anger or resentment fueled by our ethnic differences.

When I awoke the following morning, a gratifying sense coursed through me, as if their indomitable spirit still flowed within my veins even in the 21st century. I yearned for the day when they would open up about their feelings regarding the abduction and captivity enforced by their slave masters, wondering how they perceived their situation. However, in my dream interactions with them, an unspoken discomfort lingered, perhaps stemming from their unease in conversing with a stranger. I sensed their apprehension about discussing their struggles and trials. Nevertheless, their experiences were so harrowing that few could endure such torture without seeking revenge or succumbing to despair.

It is said that some slaves overheard their masters discussing the teachings of the Bible, conveying a notion that their existence would hold greater significance in the eyes of God on judgment day. In their attempts to persuade those slaves who listened, the masters proclaimed that the color of one's skin would bear no value in the divine realm.

He asserted that possessing a pure heart would be the sole means for them to witness God's acceptance into His kingdom, hoping for divine inclusion. Failure to comply with this teaching might result in dire consequences, even death. Considering the prevailing conflicts between black and white communities today, I find myself questioning the nature of the fear instilled within some white individuals, despite the fact that they are the ones often wielding guns and perpetrating violence. It is perplexing that such brutalities have persisted against black people for centuries, with little to no remorse shown for the loss of precious human lives.

Furthermore, it is difficult to comprehend how white individuals could endure such abuse for an extended period without mobilizing for a battle against their oppressors. Nevertheless, history has shown that the collective experiences of wars and hardships have failed to bring about a significant change in the way black people are treated today. Yet, in light of these ongoing issues, I hold hope that the American populace has expressed their unequivocal stance through their voting in elections. It is imperative that they vocalize their opinions regarding the democratic system and their willingness to defend it, irrespective of the political party in power, be it Democrats or Republicans. Moreover, I firmly believe that achieving greater diversity in Congress, ensuring equitable representation for all Americans, would greatly contribute to their cause.

It is truly remarkable how the diverse choices of the American people have stirred millions, resulting in the election of a Black woman as vice president and the appointment of other Black officials to Congress. This development stands out in a time where racism often seems to supersede morals and principles. Surprisingly, racism has proliferated rapidly in our nation, with little intervention from our judicial system to curb the violence. We owe a measure of gratitude to Donald J. Trump for unveiling the deep-rooted racial issues, exposing them to the world and prompting some Americans to express radical views about our collective future. This revelation has allowed us to identify those infected with this disease, which only exacerbates the distress since doctors, scientists, and ministers have yet to develop a love vaccine capable of eliminating this problem from the hearts of racists.

It is unfortunate that African Americans find themselves armed solely with pens, pencils, and their voices as they strive to defend their honor as Americans against the weapons of guns, bombs, and nuclear arsenal. After enduring centuries of patience while waiting for respect, the time has come for Black Americans to celebrate their own independence. They have endured cruelty and humiliation unjustly inherited through the years. It is essential for us to acknowledge whether we are ready or not to unite Black and White Americans and establish a recognized holiday, titled "African Americans Day," to be celebrated annually on May 3rd. This day would serve as a tribute to all dark-skinned Americans, both past and present, for their invaluable contributions to this country. It is an opportunity to honor their positive impact and rightful place in our shared history.

This holiday would hold significant meaning for people across the globe, as they come together to celebrate despite the agonies they have endured. It would serve as a testament to the courage displayed by both black and white Americans, defying the odds to establish this holiday, particularly in the face of vehement opposition. We cannot overlook the relentless efforts of Donald J. Trump and his political party, aligning themselves with the southern states' attempts to suppress the voting rights of people of color. Their success in maintaining power in these battleground states, where the Civil War was lost, poses a formidable challenge as we protest and attempt to bring attention to the rampant occurrences of murder plaguing our cities and states, seemingly falling on deaf ears.

It seems their objective is to perpetually subjugate black individuals, ensuring their dominance prevails over principles and morals. Sadly, we find ourselves relying on the future to construct a new world, one free from the false ideologies perpetuated by deceptive politicians of the past. Our aspiration is for this new world to be firmly established on the solid foundation of goodwill, where every human being can coexist peacefully. We owe a debt of gratitude to the past and present freedom fighters who endured immense suffering and gave their lives so that we could experience a semblance of freedom. Regrettably, those who fought in the Civil War and emerged victorious in the battle for freedom would likely acknowledge that the war still rages on, spanning generations and centuries, long after the Confederate Army surrendered to General Grant. It is incumbent upon me, in collaboration with politicians, to fulfill my duty by advocating for proper recognition of these individuals. I believe it is imperative to approach Congress and request the establishment of a holiday in their honor, to be known as "African Americans Day." While it is important to commemorate the lives lost tragically on 9/11 and acknowledge the history of slavery intertwined with the presidency, it is equally crucial to pay tribute to the contributions and struggles of African Americans throughout our nation's history.

Nowadays, as an Afro American who has experienced life behind bars and resides in the ghetto, the suffering of my ancestors weighs heavily on my heart. It poses a challenge for me to grapple with, as I ponder upon who among us is willing to empathize with the unimaginable cruelties inflicted upon them that still linger in our collective consciousness. Despite the passage of time, the remnants of that particular phase of slavery continue to cast a shadow over our lives. Yet, amidst the pain, I maintain a glimmer of hope.

However, if I listen hard enough, I can hear the voices from the dead whispering in my ear the melody of hope and fear, singing about a better life after death. In which at that time their only inspiration that motivated them to continue toiling in the fields was spending eternity in Heaven! Furthermore, when I was a child most of us were taught to respect our elders, or be discipline with a whip. I admit, some of us were confused about a Jewish God they prayed to for help. Still, we tried to get a better understanding of the language they used to express themselves in the Bible. Nevertheless, just out of respect for our parents we kept trying to learn more about the history, of their God and His son Jesus?

The problem is, even today what we are being taught by Ministers and Christians is the same propaganda our ancestors taught their children in the past, and even now in the 21st century. Still after all these years the Bible has kept some people doubting realistic facts proving to be contrary to the existence of Jesus and his disciples. Let me be clear, I'm not an (Agnostic). It's just difficult to believe even now some Christians refuse out of fear to have any realistic discussions about Jesus' aside of their comfort zone of faith and belief!! Scholars have written your fate was predicted by God the moment you were conceived in your mother's womb.

Hoping to exist one day with their ancestors eternally in the presence of God. We, should be prudent enough to understand from the diabolical way we've treated each other without regret! We shouldn't feel disappointed if God decide we're not worthy to be in His presence!

I know some critics will say who gave me the authority to sit in judgment of others, writing about who God will or not accept in his kingdom? When He's known to be a God who shows mercy and forgiveness? When I searched, through our history it will substantiate, jealousy is one of the main causes of death killing too many people in our span of time. Still, we claim to have a close relationship with God through our faith believing in Him! So, what is this fantasy we're teaching our children and the public everyday about their God who refuses to answer, or provide refuge for them in crisis that involves life and death? Although I realize He's the only controlling force between the past present and future. Scholars also have written, He's unlimited in power over the Universe, to change what's necessary in our experiences of life and death.

Yes, it's possible Scholars and Philosophers will probably disagree with this particular concept about God's existence because of my lack of degrees in theology. Sometimes in some of our experiences in life we become sidetracked preventing some of us to accept reality in situations like this. Because most of the theories we accept are based on our belief, and our own set of facts. That's always debatable whether it's true or not? I guess the public have a way of analyzing what's debatable concerning God or any other subject prior to what's documented by scholars. I'm not trying to start anything between them one way or the other.

Now, some of us have the tendency to remain loyal believing the same rhetoric of the past, that left us more confused about our future today than yesterday? Instead of blaming ourselves for our lack of progress voting for the same politicians hoping I'll stressful living conditions will somehow change overnight for the better. Furthermore, I believe from the length of time we've given our elected officials to change our conditions and the problems we're facing now. Shouldn't have been that challenging to solve after trying for centuries. It's time to collaborate asking our-selves how much longer will Americans continue to be the victims of politician's misuse of power?! They commit these acts of cruelty without fear of incarceration. Yeah, I know we complain about our problems and do nothing to change a system designed to keep us dependent on their laws' that enhance their wealth while the rest of us struggle to survive every day!

The threat of death continues to be advocated by some White supremacist because of their lack of vision, to make America the kind of place we brag about. Although its agonizing knowing politicians could show their support to Black people, but their greed hinders what's left of their morality to give the proper service the public deserves. However, weighing our options Americans can't afford to wait for those in power to get their act together. Now we've stepped into the Danger zone fighting against death being involved in Numerous of wars, when our foes see Americans don't always practice what they preach about equal justice under the law.

Now that we've pulled the plug out of morals and principles, and placed it in the socket of lies and deceit. It's unfortunate, some of us don't realize once that energy dies in other Countries it can't be revived! Still, with all our false we're determine to survive, providing we stop being servants to those who are privileged, knowing they always capitalize on our misfortunes. Remember, when we send our children and grandchildren to their schools to pledge their allegiance to the flag.

I've heard Critics have said, the attitude of some teachers gave some of the brightest of our children failing grades trying to obstruct them from advancing to a higher level in their studies. Especially those who understand, their ancestors built this country with their blood and sweat are the ones having these disputes with their teachers. Unfortunately, because of cases like this some of them feel subdued because they looked different from the majority of their class-mates! Now, people are concerned if politicians are willing to share American legacy with them in peace? Or die in wars filled with hate because of our Ethnic differences!

For centuries we've given credit to Gorge Washington and Abraham Lincoln and other pioneers Black and White for their structural participation. Creating Laws as the principals to guide us individually and collectively along the way to greatness! What's so heart breaking for me, that is when I look back in time and see the disadvantages that followed Black people all these years. It was like being in the midst of a raging bear trying to protect her young from intruders! Yes, intruders a word Americans use as a brand name to identify black people from White immigrants who migrated here from other Countries.

Now for the first time in years I feel optimistic that President Joe Biden will set a new standard of how all Americans should be treated. Also, I wonder what will be the consequences to make peace with those who don't recognize those who look different as being human? Would it be life or death for those who refuse to comply to Black people's aspirations to be treated as Americans? Yeah, change, a word needed for physical and spiritual growth because without it, we wouldn't have what's necessary to exist on a higher level of intellect with the understanding of who we are as Americans. Especially in this world with the kind of distinction needed to pass on to our youth.

Look, I'm not trying to be a mister know it all, I'm just trying to use common sense to stay focus, living in a world filled with hate! Yes, I know there are people who may disagree of being mistreated, because they haven't lived under these kinds of stressful conditions, being violated on every level one can imagine! Sure, most of us know what's needed in this country to change that particular concept about Black people that's taught for centuries. However, only a few Americans seems to have the courage to fight knowing their lives may be in danger. Advocating these (racial problems still exist).

We should know there are times when tough love is required in cases like this to speak truth regardless of the dangers involved. Sure, to the deviant ones who lose interest, reading about the struggles of some Black men and women. I feel the same way writing about White men murdering them for hundreds of years. Still, they have the patience to wait hoping politicians who advocate justice for all, will eventually stop trying to dehumanize people through their laws.

However, it's undeserving that I've heard Ministers from just about every denomination except from the Pope. The question is why is this leader of faith being (silent) about the conduct of evil doers without conferring his position on race? This messenger of God who supports the English translated version of the Bible, that a Black man paid for, they call it the (King James Version of the Bible).

Yet the Pope seems unprepared in commenting about what's being allowed in cruelties against Black people for hundreds of years. Sure, we understand the Pope have other world problems to consider that's just as urgent to speak about during his travels in different countries. However, I guess news casters seem to have no interest interviewing the Pope about his opinion of the continued homicides that's occurring every day. Meanwhile until he speaks on these issues their jealousy of each other continues in death.

It's inexcusable that some Americans conjure up the urge to kill different ethnic groups of people at first sight. Yet they go to their different churches every Sunday especially on Xmas and Easter void of conscience. Yes, it's unconscionable just the thought of spending eternity facing their enemies isn't a gratifying predicament to be subjected to?

Especially, associating with individuals who were the killers of your loved-ones. Can you imagine having that kind of reunion in Heaven. However, if that reunion is acceptable by their god, then I'll decline being there and take my chances not to exist at all, unless there's a better option?!! There were times living together with White people wasn't so bad until I traveled through the southern part of this country.

When I saw Black people (hanging from trees), it changed my life forever. Nevertheless, it's noticeable when there's a crisis concerning the death of Black people Fox News and other News casters broadcast their views speaking negatively about them in public. Knowing their anger and frustration was justified, after seeing their loved ones gunned down in the streets! Through the years we've seen and heard obnoxious News reporters down playing police officers acts of violence. Saying Black people kill each other more than police officers, as if that justifies killing Black people in bunches throughout the states.

Gorge Floyd is one of many examples of how some people's nonchalant attitude ignoring violence especially when an American is being killed in plain sight!! Yet I admit, after 70 years of living under the same conditions in the 1940s and 50s. Still, we're witnessing White police officers shooting people in the back unarmed!! The question is, are we prepared to face the consequences of our actions, considering our failure to legislate gun laws that will modify what's really needed to prevent gun violence. Nevertheless, rather it's negative or positive the end results will reflect our living conditions depending on our leader's concept of progress. It would be gratifying if politicians could accept facts about why Americans are tired of being used and abused, also with the judicial system. Sure, we talk about hope and justice every-day that's always standing in the shadows of possibilities and never reaches the phase of reality, for those who need reparation the most.

Unfortunately, there are people hoping and praying to be transformed to another being to escape reality, living in a mystical world after death. However, if they continue believing that philosophy, they've metaphorically lost touch with realistic facts about dying? Historically, our ancestors weren't allowed the luxury of reading and writing about America's history. Showing their superiority in weaponry and technology from other countries.

Still, Black people showed their superior strength working under conditions their oppressors wouldn't have survived under the scorching sun. Even today they are faced with the same challenges of acceptance politically and socially. Nevertheless, politicians' refusal to acknowledge facts of people being murdered, has caused skepticisms, about fairness in our Court system. Sometimes politicians flaunt justice as being blind when it involves some people's safety, and having equal opportunities to succeed. However, now people are aware of the excuse used to justify why politician's refuse to address this problem of racism without prejudice. Their excuse is they fear unarmed (Black men). Personally, what I've seen from the past seventy years nothing has changed so evidently, they must be lying! Fortunately, we've known based on the evidence, it didn't support White men's claims of being threated or attacked by the people they claim to fear.

CHAPTER 2

Why have we ignored the facts?

Through the years I've read similar stories attracting attention of Millions of people around the world. Now, it's their contention they're experiencing the same problem of racism in their countries. Yes, we've known for centuries White people are the main source used as piers to judge Black people whether they've committed a crime or not?

I hope I'm not giving the impression all White people are racist, it's just Black people's support is at a minimal from a majority of palms trying to inflect harm instead of trying to relieve the pressure. It's like my daughter Sylva said, "Dad if Americans really wanted to stop racism in this Country, they would've done it (400 years ago)" so don't sweat it. However, I wonder is there a realistic solution that will eliminate the ongoing violence of Black Americans to finally be accepted as Americans and be treated as such?

However, it's crucial that we acknowledge Black Soldier and our enemies they warred against and won fighting and dying for a cause in their countries showing their patriotism to this Country. Unfortunately, after the fighting is over, their Black sons and daughters are being disrespected, violated and killed. Either driving, jogging, or walking through their neighborhoods that's predominately White. Also, it's time to stay focus because their reaction to Black people could be deadly whether they're doing something illegal or not?

Furthermore, our statistics in gun violence reveal 90 per-cent of crimes committed against Americans are either police officers, or White civilians. Carrying weapons walking in schools and other places killing people. Obviously, we've waited too long to clamp down on White supremacist who indulge in committing murder. Can you believe at this point in time, our system is ready to accept more White foreigners without further investigation of them being considered as full Americans. For them it's simple, not having a criminal record, and if they agree to certain stipulations by making a pledge to this Country. Also, passing a written test studying the History of this Country, then according to our laws they've done what's required to be accepted as American citizens!!

Now, they've grown accustom thinking Millions of Black people are mostly concern about an afterlife, instead of negotiating a better future here in America? For centuries, we've ignored how their Christian philosophies effects the minds people, Black and White? Still, some of us kill each other while teaching Christianity exposing the public to deadly events ruining the lives of future generations of our children. Making them further confused if it's better to live or die to find refuge for eternity?

Let's not be (naive), listening to reporters saying how brave the police were, even after they were told the people, they killed weren't armed. Still, after all these years the courts are vigorously persistent in denying protection of Black people giving them the opportunity to protect and defend their-selves in a crisis.

For years we've seen politicians smiling faces during their political speeches saying they stand for justice for all Americans. This charade of killings will never stop, if we ignore the fundamental principles by which we live, not allowing criminals to commit Murder against any American White or Black? Instead, we're teaching our children about a life or world after death, that neither of us have experienced physically? However, just having faith isn't enough evidence to justify the existence of an unseen spiritual world to people who understand realistic facts! Nevertheless, someone should check those theologians who concur confusing people saying, they believe this spiritual world exist.

Still, it brings more doubt to sceptics especially without some physical evidence being discussed in a logical manner to prove mystical citizens will exist physically somewhere in an unknown world. They seem to believe having faith will sustain them, without realizing they've been misled, spiritually for Centuries. If only their Ancestors had evidence to prove their slave masters were lying using a Jewish spiritual Doctrine to deceive them from knowing the truth? It might've changed the concept of what we believe to-day.

Still, I wait hoping before I expire in this life, reality will be confirmed in the mind of the weak to acknowledge facts without being persuaded to think otherwise. I personally would like to know, who's qualified to lead them in a direction that will guide them safely to their destination? Further traveling on a journey to reach a city that hasn't been explored physically by any creature known to man. Especially when their charts of directions are limited to, North, South, East, and West, or going up or down. Furthermore, why not ask yourself is it logical to believe the grave is really the pathway to Heaven, I believe some Christians will say yes although they are limited physically to prove it?

Even if it's possible to accomplish it beneath the ground, isn't the route I would choose to travel, even if I believed most of what scholas wrote in the Bible. It's astounding why my people continue to believe this mythical religious tradition our ancestors were forced to accept under the whip? Now we have the opportunity to make our own choices if what they're teaching the world is logical to believe or disbelieve without being criticized for having our own way thinking. Knowing the method, they used to force our Ancestors to submit their will hoping they can live again physically after death.

It's amazing, we should know better after reaching maturity realizing we're not children anymore, listening to a bed time story taught to us by our parents. Although I must admit it has a fascinating ending, just like most fairytales, if they chose to believe their philosophy. However, it was also written in the Bible, when I was a child, I thought as a child, but when I became a man, I put away (childish things)! I know it's hard not conforming to traditions of the past, but we're not slaves anymore. Suffering, from the chains our ancestors wore wrapped around their ankles and their necks.

Especially around the necks of those brave Black men and women who rebelled trying to escape, tired of waiting for their White master Jesus to rescue them from the hang man's rope. Yeah, we still believe those written words said in the Bible about Jesus dying for us. It's no doubt some Christians reading this book might say this Devils book about Jesus is very disrespectful. Even when he promised his disciples saying he's coming back for them, without mentioning if the rest of us were included?

Moreover, if you don't believe this spiritual Doctrine was designed to mislead and distract people from knowing the truth. Then I regret my inability to reach the logical part of your mind to think realistically about what's written in the Bible. Knowing, our ancestors couldn't question the Bible with skepticism without risking their lives to have that privilege, feels me with anguish. I guess it's because when White men forced them to read the Bible, claiming they were less than (Three-Fifths) of a man. politicians didn't know they would rise above their scrutiny to achieve legislation that saves people's lives. Although we were taught by Jesus if someone slaps you on one check turn the other.

However, now it's different we're living in a system that made it lawful if you're attacked by anyone, you can defend your-self. Nevertheless, they seem to be dedicated trying to influence Christians to believe and accept the Bible as God's word. Well in case you didn't know, in their teaching's they made it clear the (Jews) were God's chosen people! Those were the challenges Black people had to live with as part of their system that's degrading others who read that book. Listening to them indicating through their Bible the Gentiles were less favorable even in the eyes of God, that's why some of them feel superior to others?

However, after being stripped of their African heritage to practice their own religious beliefs. Nevertheless, hearing that kind of threat anyone would've adhered to their master Jesus whether they believed in him or not? I know some religious critics will say it doesn't matter if he's Black or White, because they've had some spiritual encounters with Jesus. Some people were overwhelmed, after he spoke or touched them in an unfamiliar manner they can't explain. My question is, why he didn't reveal himself to them before they knew he (existed)?

Moreover, I hate to be the one to sit in judgment of anyone's spiritual experiences because I was raised in the same environment. However, I'm proud to say this is no scheme to mislead anyone about the Bible, what I'm searching for is the truth. Now it has finally come to the surface and some truth tellers are not afraid to write or speak it to the public, saying they were deceived about the afterlife. All I'm asking is please take the time and finish reading this book, it might change the way you feel about reading the facts.

Instead of being a skeptic believing a philosophy that keeps you doubtful of what you've heard or read. Traveling to different churches not being completely satisfied with the message from Ministers in the past? Searching for the truth, or should I be reminded that some people can't handle the (truth)? It seems when people's minds go beyond logic in a spiritual debate. Their answers to a realistic question, seems so mystifying, that it wanders in uncharted territories, and their minds become lost in the aftermath of reason! Hold on to that thought, because it seems they've allowed their belief and faith in the Bible to be an absolute religious doctrine.

Ministers have said Satan's evil spirit walks and talks with us on a daily basis. Unfortunately, politicians' purpose is to dominate our good will behavior. This can happen unknowingly because we've allowed them to control our mind, to be used to keep us servants, instead of masters of our own will to decide if we should follow facts or fiction? It seems we're afraid to admit, at times we fall victims of their diabolical thoughts of hate, which we know makes us incapable to think realistically about the problems we're facing every-day.

Well, we know according to the Bible, God's chosen people the Jews renounces that accusation of Jesus being God's begotten son, according to their records! Obviously, it's all part of some Christians strategy to influence the gullible to gain their support financially. Now people are skeptical, about praying to God for answers to stop this force of evil, or should they take it upon their selves to act according to the Law to stop the anger? Even when our records indicate their laws has failed Americans for centuries looking for justice? Or are they compelled to honor their White mentors this way by killing different ethnic groups of Americans, trying to remind them they're still their Masters?

If that's true, we haven't changed from stalling, to put an end to this horror of injustice that continue to control us through fear and ignorance of the facts! Now their becoming bolder in their aggression, because of their lack of fear of being killed, when committing these acts of murder? Now for the first time I'm hearing News Casters complaining about being replaced with a new look of colorful people, being hired to express a new version of reporting. However, now people are having a different version of reporting from those we've heard in the past, expressing their views about racism. It seems to be unpopular when they're confronted with threats of death, while doing their job when they separate facts from fiction.

Critics are saying some reporters are afraid of progress, is it because their reporting lacks credibility to their viewers on racial issues? It's about time Americans are, realizing Black people aren't safe in this country. Especially, if life and death circumstances remain the same, when law-makers don't confront their problems serious enough to stop the violence. It makes Blacks more concerned about their youth growing up witnessing such devastation between White and Black Americans. Now, they're being forced to live in stressful situations knowing their youth becomes vulnerable to future events that may cause more violence.

Actually, if an eighteen-year-old White boy can own guns to kill innocent children, why can't Black children be armed to defend themselves against anyone trying to kill them? Why is it when Black people use those words in Court, I feared for my life, it seems (meaningless) to those men and women who's judging their cases? Unfortunately, when Black people kill being attacked defending their-self against White police officers, they're still convicted of murder regardless of the evidence proving they were justified! Obviously, you can't explain what happened if you're (dead), or do their lives have less value because some jerk is wearing a police uniform?

There was a time back in the old west, I was told when predators shoot unarmed people Black or White in the back, they were considered cowards, whether they wore a Badge or not. Now, the court have reversed that decision in their courts saying when the police kill's unarmed people, they're justified and in the line of duty, when Black men and women are the victims of foul play! It's a shame police officers who were assigned to serve and protect the American people against armed men at the Capital. We saw their refusal to fire their weapons in self-defense is really baffling to say the least?

Now in this situation at the Capital, it was different, when they didn't hold their ground against those thugs with guns, believe me that's real fear!! Nevertheless, that's not being reported now. It would be unforgivable if we've forgotten the tragedy years ago? When we couldn't save one of our youths from being killed unarmed on his way home by a vigilante, who wasn't convicted of killing him. (Why), because the killer said the young man looked suspicious of committing a crime after he bought a box of skittles at a neighborhood store? We know Palms are protected with millions of guns, so there's no way young Black men can stay alive against these threats of violence without being armed?

This is important to create awareness especially when they're dealing with a coward with a gun, who have no conscience concerning if Black people live or die! I hope that lesson of death is being taught to Black men, waiting for their elected officials to defend their families in court. There seems to be an older generation of Black mentors giving advice to people of what actions to take in a crisis. It's kind of tragic, after 400 years the only advice I'm hearing from their leaders who refuse to change their advice, telling them to be patient until Congress is ready to adhere to their demands.

Meanwhile thousands of people are still dying from (police violence). However, when I saw some of those videos on TV, it was heartbreaking witnessing that kind of defense Black people used against these acts of murder. They were holding up signs that read (Black Lives Matter) knowing these murderers don't feel the same sentiment to stop killing them. I hope in the future these young and older entertainers will spread the message through their music, exposing a system that's allowing an undeclared death sentence of being Black in America. Hollywood producers have created movies showing their version of what happened to Black people in the 16th century, and even now.

Telling their version of changing the names of their ethnic background to their slave master's last name, showing ownership of them. For centuries Black people have shown a sense of pride passing their slave masters last name to their children and grandchildren. However, we know that's no longer necessary because those rules don't apply in the 21st century. Really, it's time to admit carrying our enemies last names, has been a curse instead of a blessing!

Unfortunately, we've lost the urge to teach our children a lesson in the value, of being who they are knowing who their DNA belongs to, and the African names that goes with their Heritage! They should know, not acknowledging where their ancestors came from it's a disservice to their blood line. That should indicate they're violating their birth right although they're still African Americans. Trying, to show respect by using the last names of people who hung their ancestors, isn't necessary to stay alive anymore.

Unfortunately, when Palms see you're reluctant to reveal your true identity, they laugh at you, until you free yourself of everything that blocks out your true identity. Even if you start over Culturally, accepting the truth by renaming your-selves prop-erly, creating a blueprint for the next generation to follow. Yes, don't wait, the future of your race is anxious to be discovered with an African name! Seriously, it's time making that effort your priority to search through your DNA consistently until you find some evidence of your heritage and where you came from?!

Then choose a name from their language and sustain it for Centuries, like your ancestors did with the names you're using now to be identified. Not unless someone has a better method to regain your true (identity). Spending years serving in their Military making them richer in this Country, know-ing their family members can barely survive on a Welfare check. It seems when Black people show pride in serving, or dying in battle isn't enough for some Americans who refuse to reveal their identity to the public, refusing to show their African faces as heroes on the News.

Okay I admit, it's hard for me to stop writing about this subject from the lack of interest shown concerning the problems some Americans face every-day)!! Especially, when they're sending a mes-sage to the world people of different colors have no value, unless they're in an arena playing basketball, or performing in other areas of entertainment! I guess if some people had the ability to astound the world in their professional career's they wouldn't have need of Black people being here.

It's sad and obvious once they leave the arena or the stages they were performing on. They become to some Americans just another nigger on the loose wondering around in their communities. However, we should know by now, it doesn't matter what Black people engage in, dedicating their lives to be accepted, they will always be the victims of White predators if they're not armed!!

Furthermore, I believe the word kill or killed seems synonymous with the word hate. Obviously, you would have to hate someone with a great deal of animosity to annihilate them, unless it's proven to be in self-defense. Now these immigrants come here stressed and begging for help, now some of them insinuate because they're White they are superior to everyone else. Which causes animosity pretending Black people are not citizens after dodging bullets, and the hangman's rope, just to live here in peace. Who else would be more qualified according to endurance to be an American. Especially after they fought in their wars/carrying the work load for hundreds of years, without politicians showing them respect or gratitude for still being patriotic!!

Through the years we've ignored the pressure our young people are facing, walking a tight rope trying to stay out of prison. Still, they show courage, trying to navigate through abhorrent conditions knowing it mean nothing to those who's privileged if they succeed or fail. While others who work hard every day, they're children are dying because they can't afford Health insurance. That's why a lot of Americans are exhausted trying to survive, listening to the same rhetoric that's not helping them or their families succeed.

Still, our children are being taught by their teachers who will have more privileges in this Country than their Black students after they graduate. These children know what they're teaching doesn't reflect or abolish the threats on their lives in their communities. I'm not trying to suggest they're asking for pity; they just want what's being denied to them and millions of Americans, and that's justice. So much is happening with their relatives, and their neighbors being killed, and suffering from the Corona-virus. Those are the vicissitude that makes it harder for our youth to concentrate in school!!

Just think about when Black children see their mothers and Fathers who spent 12 years navigating through the educational system. Seeing them fail to accomplish their dreams, with their salaries that can barely pay their bills including food and rent. Yeah, when you live through those kinds of conditions at home, it really doesn't motivate a lot of them to participate in school assignments.

CHAPTER 3

Another Way of Drowning

That's when their trouble starts at home, when Black children in the ghetto see other children with launch money every-day. They can't buy the item's they're craving to eat; they start acting aggressive against other children with money. Forcing those children to respond trying to protect themselves which may cause physical injury to one or more of them! Now depending on the injury and the age of the child that's responsible for the injuries, it could lead to criminal charges against both of them. Then their identity is exposed to a difference experience dealing with the police and the judicial system! Which has a different set of rules for White and Black Americans. To intimidate especially Black children by raising their voices, sometimes using profanity to get a negative reaction. While threatening to take them to jail if they don't confess to crimes most of them didn't commit.

Which is opposite with White children, police officers will speak with a softer tone using a fatherly technique calling them son to ease the tension between them! Why would these law enforcement agencies send White police officers to Black communities, if they're not trying to create more tension between them? Especially when they're claiming to be afraid of them? However, until they see some changes in their conduct toward Black people, then we're see some positive results in communicating with them. If the system doesn't have enough Black police officers to patrol communities that's predominantly Black, then they should raise their percentage of recruiting Black people before this problem gets worse!!

What's so disturbing about this episode of murders, they call themselves honorable citizens and connected to Christian families? Which makes me wonder if they're reading a different Bible from the rest of us. Further making the impression their Jesus isn't concerned about what happens to the people they said he died, so they could have eternal life? Unfortunately, no one knows if God will punish them now while they're living or wait until they're deceased to pass judgment to those responsible for the continued deaths of Black people everywhere?

It would appear, punishing someone after their dead would be a waste of time to the victims who want to see justice now? Obviously, that's not our call to make according to their Bible, but to wait for Gods final decision to judge the dead. If it's possible He's decided to wait until all of us dies before He passes judgement of over 400 years of crimes against Black people and others.

I know many of us won't understand the logic in that approach, especially if their God is willing to forgive them of their sins against humanity? However, some critics are expressing their views and the attitude of those men in Congress concerning Black American's. I quote, "politicians don't consider Black people as Americans, they still consider them as freed slaves without owners". Sure, I was a little shaken by that commit about some of our elected officials, still I couldn't argue against their views!! Now consider what would've happen if the situation was reversed against Palms for over 400 years of torment?

Unfortunately, our records indicate when Black people need assistance to provide refuge for them in a life-or-death situation, it seems no one is willing to assist them physically in their defense. Furthermore, we know our loved ones have sacrificed their lives for many years hoping for the same protection privileged Americans receive. Moreover, what they hope for is not necessarily guaranteed if they're not sucking somebody's prostate gland to get it.

Some people ask how can we change the metaphor politicians are advocating to the public. Obviously, it seems those who want change might be forced to violence, trying to accomplish it the way the late Mr. Malcolm X suggested, by any means necessary!! I would love if people stop listening to unsubstantiated propaganda that's causing so much division. However, it's never too late to start over when we're headed in the wrong direction. It's time to acknowledge we have a purpose, instead of acting in ways that's unbecoming to us as Americans.

Furthermore, let's not forget, there's only one race and that's the (Human Race)!! Sure, we've all made plenty mistakes in the past and that's okay as long as the effort is made to correct them with sincerity! Just think about all the unnecessary deaths we've caused that could've been avoided, if only we had a different mindset toward each other. Yes, I know we've had a lot of difficult challenges to overcome most of our lives, so this isn't a new story we haven't read before!! However, whether we choose to admit it or not, most of us carry the same last names of their forefathers in which makes us related to some degree, if not by family members, we still should feel a sense of being connected as Americans.

Unfortunately, I know there will be a minority group who will choose to go backward in time, instead of feeling energized to go forward. Unfortunately, these politicians seem to have something different in mind, that's causing grief to a lot of families. The question is, can Americans put aside this kind of change that's threatening our Democracy causing political problems reversing love into hate? Now for the first time in years I feel optimistic about our future relationships as Americans, because of our new leader president Joe Biden.

Now we have a chance to carry equality across the goal line, or fumble the effort because we've been hit hard by our opponent Donald Trump. It's obvious he's trying to prevent Black people from crossing over to finally being appreciated for who they are (genetically). Yes, we understand this isn't easy to change, when you're fighting this kind of war without using guns for protection, when the difference is their freedom only exist on a piece of paper.

Nevertheless, if Congress refuses to enforce the rules, justice will not prevail for all of our citizens!! If some Americans consider life as a game believe me, they're playing by the wrong rules, to win from their opposition which is politicians who feel they're superior to others! Moreover, if we allow these people to control the game of life then politicians win automatically, because we're playing by their rules instead of ours.

They use different strategies to confuse their opponents, by turning them against each other, while controlling the game of combat to work in their favor. Now critics are saying we've allowed them to succeed, out of our ignorance by allowing their lies to control the future. That's the strategy politicians are focused on, keeping us wondering who's responsible for our abhorrent condition God or our fellow man? I know we've heard Christians and Ministers saying, "one day God will destroy the world by fire". If that's true, we should follow the evidence from the actions of people of the world who seem to be tired of waiting for their demise!

It's no doubt if this mind set continues, we're headed for a head on collision with a different kind of fate, which is (Hell on Earth). Unfortunately, they're still believing, their Rulers are superior to different Ethnic groups of people in America and abroad? This dangerous mindset goes against their forefather's vision of how we should treat members of the human race. For years some people have known they weren't included when they wrote the statement about, all men are created equal. Nevertheless, although they didn't (practice) what they said at that time, those words are true.

We should keep in mind this materialistic world we're living in is only limited to our life span here on Earth. It's a place to enjoy in peace while we occupy this space in time, not to destroy each other because of (envy, jealousy or money). Nevertheless, while we're here we have the opportunity to bring life on this planet for a divine purpose to show humility to the one who created us.

It's unfortunate some politicians abuse their power in Congress and the Sovereignty they represent to the world by acting political in their judgement that's killing other human-beings. However, those who haven't heard what some politicians are saying, that's definitely in question, about some of them being above the law? No one should have the right telling Americans what their false are without considering first the devastation in the world they've created!! Nevertheless, it's still within our grasp to create the kind of curriculum that abolishes hate of every American, if they're willing to follow the rules of all men are created equal. I hope that's not (wishful thinking on their part without showing some positive results).

Sure, there might be critics who will laugh when they read this narrative saying, it won't be accomplished during their lifetime. Well, most Americans have demonstrated through the years their resilience in getting things done against the odds. Its obvious criticism is not a handicap when one shows determination in their efforts to succeed. I'm thankful to have lived long enough to witness a change in our history being fulfilled by prophets from the past, saying we shall overcome.

Nevertheless, I like acknowledging for the record, Mr. Barack, Obama the first Black President of the United States in 2008. Plus, Ms. Kamala Harris, the first Black woman vice President in 2021, and, the first Black woman Ms. Ketanji Brown Jackson a member of the Supreme Court in 2022. If only all Americans young and old could see a positive future with each other by collaborating our differences with the intent to move forward on this long journey to defeat this problem of inequality. If we succeed in that effort, it would take us to a place in America we thought wouldn't be possible. Further, having a chance of living the possibility of creating a new pathway to Heaven on Earth. Which could be a miraculous experience to witness here in (human form). Furthermore, living in this world of evolution, we've migrated a long way to reach this point in time.

Suddenly I was inspired thinking, when men women and children look in the mirror, they're looking at a miracle performed by the Creator. Especially, noticing they have different looks/shapes, and attitudes in which becomes part of their personality. It also distinguishes them being different and unique in structure, and in character. I Hope, the future will produce a diverse Congress that understands what's necessary to change these politicians that's creating this type of division among us. Now it's time for Americans to be grateful because of the sacrifices their ancestors made trying to survive in this Country to fulfill our purpose in life.

It's unfortunate there were Americans and politicians' and others, who were more concerned about the color of their skin, instead of accepting their humanity the way God created them! Showing their inner strength to the world, makes me proud their fear of being killed didn't prevent them from being the best at what they tried to accomplish. In sports Boxing, Baseball, Soccer, Football, also in Track, Even Golf. They excelled also in entertainment, Singing Dancing, Acting, Soul Music, Rap Music, Opera, Jazz, and so many other fields if they were allowed to participate.

They've also engaged in fighting wars helping to free others from Slavery, mentally or physically. Although they were still treated horribly, and unappreciated by their own Country, they still performed as champion conquering the task in front of them. Seriously, I'm not writing this book to complain it's just to bring awareness to those who's misinformed about Black people's (courage to survive)!! The only mystery is, why haven't our relationships gotten better from the length of time they've served? It's obvious after (400) plus years they're still rocking in the same boat holding on for survival from the high waves of discrimination.

The truth is only God knows if we're survive these strong currents of depression, that life throws at us individually, or drown from these violent storms of hate? Now that President Joe Biden is in office, it looks like hope is on the rise for all Americans!! He's become a breath of fresh air from the file stench of death of the past leaving Millions of Americans in mourning from the Corona-virus!! Now while I'm on the subject about death, makes me wonder if my Ancestors became Angels being rewarded for their beliefs in their White master Jesus, after being freed from their pain and suffering through death?

For years I've advocated this so-called Justice for all is only a myth. I hope it won't continue to be taught to our children by their mothers and Fathers without having lawful and physical proof that Justice exists worldwide. Unfortunately, if we continue to believe Justice exist without proof, then it's not logical to indulge in wishful thinking. Especially when politicians' actions are delaying the courts to solve this problem proved otherwise?

Now, American's are investing Millions of dollars to pioneer in places they can't survive without the proper gear? Obviously, these politicians aren't satisfied making this planet a living Hell for their citizens here. However, for years the American people still invest in projects they don't benefit from a financial point of view. (Why?) I guess it's because politicians say we're all in this together, when we know that's not true Metaphorically speaking? Furthermore, the signs are there to recognize why the creator made these boundaries filling other parts of the Universe with gases to prevent travel.

Still, we travel in space in spite of being warned, traveling through these restricted areas, invading the Creators private domain? I predict, if they continue being defiant traveling where they don't belong, it will eventually result in their demise. From the difficulty to reach these places you would think they might get the message, their journey into the unknown is forbidden? Remember the old saying about curiosity killing the (cat)? Now, when I think about their space adventures, I refuse to be distracted trying to stay focused on our immediate problems here.

Even at my age of 82, I still recognize the dangers trying to achieve what politicians ignored. Knowing, it could cost the life of Millions of Americans rebelling if they succeed? Now when I wake up in the morning, I feel relieved from the different attitudes of the American people wanting to see action from our leaders. Especially when they're failing to face facts offered to them with humility saying what Americans need!

CHAPTER 4

It's Time to Lock These Officers Up!

It's no secret, we've known through the years the reign of injustice against the American people was accepted by politicians, although what they're doing will no longer be tolerated. Now, for those who participated, without being concerned about other Americans, it's their time to pay the piper, for the debt owed to the murdered victims and their families. For violating their rights under the premise of stress, who served this Country with their lives without hesitation. Now they're dying simply because someone wearing a police uniform can lie saying they're afraid of them while they're unarmed.

My records indicate those police officers, haven't showed any emotion or empathy for what they've done killing some of the family members of their Black comrades in war. You, tell me if this is justice to allow these Monsters who's still living in their communities protected by the same police officers that's killing other Tax payers with darker skin. If that's justice then brace yourself for what's coming next. Now we expect our children Black and White to pledge their a-legion to a flag that gives some of them and their families no protection under the law?

If Americans cared about what's happening to Black people, they can prove it by stopping the violence now. Further, giving their support helping to create a Holiday once a year on the 3rd of May, (African Americans Day). It could revolutionize the way some people think about other Americans in a positive way, showing more respect for each other on that day. However, if necessary, we should take a lesson from the Jews, they don't ask the Government's permission to celebrate their Holidays. They close their businesses on that date every year, until the Government recognizes the importance of what that day means to them. However, Black people should at least have the courage to make that sacrifice on their own to acknowledge that Holiday with or without politicians' permission. To further honor collectively their own people past and present who've Sacrificed in my view, more privileges being here than anyone in this Country to be an American.

Through the years I've learned and people can believe this or not. So far, it's always' politicians' tradition to wait until Black people are dead or dying before they give them any recognition on a consistent basis. Whether it's the work load on their backs or being champions Athletically, Musically, also Inventors with their positive ideas to present to the public! Actually, some people feel based on politician's prior record they haven't earned the right to prevent Americans from celebrating whom or whatever they choose.

Especially if politicians are trying to punished them by blocking them legislatively from voting, and other Health privileges that helps them on a daily basis! Some Americans feel it's time they write their own legacy in words of truth, without reading a dialogue written by Historians who's twisting the facts about Black history to gain wealth! For too long it was tolerated, and ignored to mislead the public, without physically being taught a lesson them-selves in foul play. (This backlash) of vengeance against our citizens shouldn't be tolerated, people are tired of writing and reporting about these ongoing tragedies.

Now politicians feel frustrated because Americans are finally aware of the truth about what they're doing? Still, we fight and sometimes fail trying to reconnect with their better Angles, who can release the tension, bringing minds together in a peaceful way? It seems Black people are always, listening to criticism for being devoted sharing the responsibility to root out corruption everywhere. It's also imperative to lock up officers of the court if necessary, including judges, and investigate them in every phase of our criminal system, making it plain no one is above the law. Some Americans are afraid, hoping they haven't contaminated the principles of fair play in the Courts?

It's also time to expose conspirators who conspired with judges and lawyers accepting bribe money, allowing murderers to escape punishment for their disregard for human life. Yes, I know we've read and talked about these conditions of injustice that's always hidden from the public. Telling Black people, they're Americans and shouldn't be axile from all the benefits America has to offer through our judicial system!

I hope Americans made it clear, if we expect Justice, it shouldn't be placed totally in the hands of the majority of people who can't be trusted with people lives. Especially when their prior records indicate, some of them can't adjust according to the evidence presented in Court to render a guilty verdict! Now, people are saying this deadly assault didn't escalate to this level until the American people elected a Black man as president, which allowed his family to have residence in the White House. Yes, I wrote it, because these people whose committing these acts of Murder are sending a powerful message. I believe with the help of politicians, showing their defiance against all Americans through their actions of instigating, and committing violence.

They were heard saying, they will not relinquish their White privileges regardless of who dies in wars to defend this country. It's also tragic knowing in their statement, they won't respect any minority Black President male or female who may be staying in the White House for a short time. Now these killings are just the beginning of a fight we haven't indulged in or seen being engineered by an ex-President of the United States. So, I'm asking Americans how does it feel to get a glimpse of the future. When some Americans can't distinguish the difference between patriots and traitors who's perpetrating treason in plain sight! I believe this movement against our constitution is the priority of those elected officials.

Now the question is, are we willing to take a pragmatic approach to ashore future generations won't be subjected to these types of issues, politics and racism?!! Or are we going to wage a continuum of war against each other to ensure every American can have the same privileges as others? You know it's dreadful how hypocritical some Americans are when their history indicates, some of their ancestors migrated to this country looking for freedom from their oppressors in other countries. Now, through our Black ancestors' deaths and hard work, Millions of them are still benefiting from their survival being here!!

However, I've wondered if mankind has reached the point of being reincarnated at birth as an evil force roaming the Earth? The question is how long will this new breed of Human animals live to control the future of America? Further, we should remember this minority leader Mr. Trump was advocating to Americans during the Corona-virus, to inject Bleach in their bodies as a cure from the Virus. Yet millions of Americans follow him without questioning his motives for misleading the public.

Now he refuses to retract that deadly statement which could've killed more Americans if they were gullible enough to believe him. So, if that's what being an American looks like, then I declined to be one!! Although I assume according those republicans, when Donald Trump misled the public, no laws were broken? Obviously, they're not paying attention to the warning signs on this road filled with his dying believers, believing he should rule the world? However, if they insist on following Mr.

Trump, it should give anyone reason to turn around and head in another direction. Nevertheless, there will be people who prefer to follow those who make a fortune misleading the public, then follow politicians who's trying to save lives?

I refuse to lose faith because of possibilities that even the most racist person in America has a purpose for being here. It's always a chance his or her purpose is to change from a negative way of thinking about people, to a positive way of advocating their cause for equality. Change is a very powerful word which keeps the universe in motion whether you feel it's negative or positive in movement. Still, it affects everything and everybody who exist within the realm of the will of God. Sometimes these Universal changes influences us to act violent if we don't try to control our emotions.

You know some times it can be from anxiety, in which has affected everyone to some degree in different ways! Only you can decide which direction you're compelled to follow, those who've been mistreated or those who's trying to tear this country apart? Please remember (A Chance to Learn), will be my 4th book published. (The Minister Who Turned Gangster), (That Beastly Frame), and (Shenoi the Angel of Knowledge) are the rest" in my efforts to make contact with the public! Check them out if you have time. If not through a publishing company. You can contact me if you'd like an Autographed copy, Email me. (gilbertsamuel631@gmail.com)

(Or, leave your name and phone number), or use this contact number. (347 777 6801) for more information. However, to be fair those who are placed in Authority shouldn't be the ones to pass judgement of the status of this country, unless they're speaking from experience of being Black in America. If only the dead who were murdered under those tribal conditions could speak. I'm sure what they would say would be a lot different from what we're seeing and reading now from the press. Well, it's because a lot of Black history isn't taught in their schools. Therefore, obviously they've chosen to ignore the beginning of Human life? Which all of us should pay our respects, by honoring those who gave birth to the first Human-beings on this planet?

According to (Archaeologist and scientist), it was in a place called Africa, that's what Americans refuse to teach in their schools to our children. There might be people who are surprised reading about this in this book, still it's documented by researchers how life started with a Black man and woman giving birth to human life. Some people may ask why this part of history isn't taught in our educational system? Nevertheless, I think it's very important everyone should know where they came from just for the record? Furthermore, it's debated through evolution how a variety of different kinds of humans were developed around the world in a different assortment sizes, shapes and colors!!

I know writing about this as a reminder, will probably cause a lot of controversy and rebellion for those who don't want Black history exposed to the world. Furthermore, if you're a logical thinking person you will concur the probability of White couples producing a Black baby (is genetically impossible). However, having some experience in Art, I know different colors that's created started from the color (Black). So, these facts should indicate those who refuse to acknowledge the truth are simply responding in an irrational manner!! No one can be better than the source by which they came from, they can be equal in different ways but not better!

We should know being upset about something you've believed for years that wasn't true, doesn't change the facts about the narratives I'm writing about. From what I've seen I understand why this information won't change your position of disbelief at this time! Nevertheless, if you did the research about the History of Black people, I'm sure you'll agree these words are Historically true. I believe people know why our educational system is reluctant to teach the truth about Black history to our children Black and White, other than being slaves hundreds of years ago?

Trust me, life didn't begin with (Gorge Washington and Abraham Lincoln). They were Just like other warriors before them, they fought and conquered other Countries. Once you've learned more, you're realize that's only a small portion of the History of the Human race. The way I remember when I was going to school in the early and late 1940s and 50s. Those battles White men were engaged in, were mostly taught to White and Black children here in America. They didn't teach them the names of other warriors unless their Generals were defeated by Americans Soldiers.

It seems they are always trying to show their superiority over other people by introducing fictional characters including Superman/Wonder woman just to mention a few. Although we know those fictional characters are only a figment of their imagination, even the son of their god is (White)? I believe this is the results of what they're taught as a child! For hundreds of years, we've been too lenient for politicians to pass the test. Does the evidence show they deserve a passing grade to help people, or an (F) in their work ethics to solve their problems? It seems we've ignored teaching our children about the brunt Slaves had to endure for centuries. It might make a difference in their attitude toward people when they become adults.

Hopefully, then you're consider how tired they were going through such agony for hundreds of years without anyone changing their conditions? Yes, through all their suffering every day, Palms have to be reminded that (Black lives matters)? So, if by chance you're not capable through your conscience to show empathy for what those people experienced in life? Then sadly you're not the type of American I'm trying to reach in this book! Furthermore, I don't think it's appropriate if some of our politicians and the American people feel they're above reproach for the crimes some of them committed?

If you feel they're above reproach then in my opinion you've lost what's required by the laws of ethics your lack of respect for other human-beings? Even now I can feel my ancestor's spirit still crying out for justice not for their-self, it's for those who've been forgotten! Nevertheless, if new ground can be broken to solve this dilemma of being hated, it would make the world a better place. Also, it would ensure what it means to conquer our negative instincts that seem to last as long as we exist, if we're not willing to change our devastating rules of conduct!

Which proves to people who've read the Bible, it indicated Hell will be our next destination, if we fail to abide by its rules in this life. Which is supposed to prepare us to live eternally with God in the next life. Or are we limited by the forces of Evil that plagues our good intentions like a virus causing death which will eventually destroy our purpose for being here. I won't deny they've been theories claiming the creator uses us on an individual bases, according to our assignments given from the length of time He's allowed us to exist according to His mercy. However, one evening I was confronted with questions asking if God is a man or a woman, making these decisions if we exist or not? (Sure, it was an unusual question to consider)?

However, I don't think anyone really knows if God is male or female? I must admit our concept about God is only (theory), is the response I gave to the question. Although, it's my understanding according to this system and the books I've read. I assume God's masculinity was based on their studies from biblical scalars. Also, calling God our Father in their prayers to describe His origin? I guess scalars were using the same principle of the way a woman was created from a man helping to give birth to another being. Sure, there are millions of people who believe one of Adam's ribs was extracted from his body and placed in another form, calling its first name (woo)-and its last name-(man).

Now, based on that theory I know I'll get a lot of feedback and that's Okay to discuss it. Now according our records Millions of people know the Bible, has dominated in sales around the world. Trying to convince the public and Christians that Heaven does exist somewhere in this massive Universe? I won't get too deep in this analysis right now about their God because it's a very sensitive topic to discuss. It seems the problem is those who know and read the Bible from Ministers to politicians and people of faith can't find Carmon ground in their discussions with politicians to solve this problem of racism around the world.

Nevertheless, I was told by critics, saying the Pope could play a major part speaking about his understanding about race. Especially, when they hear his views on that subject it could make a huge difference in people's pondering over the truth. I know this racial problem is still affecting the way we see each other, based on our religious beliefs and faith that what's in the Bible is true. (Why)? What happened to their morals and principles when they're not worshiping in their sanctuaries/synagogues or in churches on Saturdays and Sundays? Furthermore, if we really believe in God, it would be prudent if we take a moment and reflect on the future, and consider how to fight our foes more effectively without participating in violence.

You can believe it or not, I'm still waiting to hear the views from the Pope sharing his wisdom, if their White Jesus existed physically or not? If not, it would change the hold concept of Christianity, and their communions in memory of Jesus death. Further, if Jesus did exist physically, the Pope would definitely know if he was Black or White during that era? Either way it's time for all of us to know about Jesus real identity, it probably would help us accept each other the way we all were created from divine love?

However, being secretive about Jesus could make their religion more dangerous than other religious doctrines. Yes, I know telling the truth has its danger points when people act scared when they hear the truth!! However, that's the reason it's so important to know why the Pope isn't eager to answer these questions that keeps us afraid to be united. He knows these problems exist, makes me feel suspicious that something's missing in the Bible we have yet to discover?

Now, it's obvious they use silence as their defense to avoid commenting on controversial issues dealing with Black History? Well, it's not much difference if you're brave enough to track their records, it seems similar when the Republicans were silent, allowing Mr. Trump to plant the seed of doubt saying ex-president Obama wasn't an American citizen? It's time to admit how republicans refused to tell the truth until the proof of his birth was so over-whelming, they had to confess Mr. Trump accusations, about Mr. Obama weren't true. Also, it doesn't seem to bother Mr. Mitch McConnell a republican acting like he has more influence in the Senate than the president of the United States?

He had the audacity to be bold enough to tell Americans he's going to block what the president is trying to accomplish, to help Americans survive this crisis. Still these republicans' men and women young and old are acting bolder carrying the confederate flag in the Capital demonstrating and showing their power to the world as insurrectionist. Moreover, we should be asking these politicians, why a lie isn't a criminal offense, when Millions of people died and still dying without knowing the truth? Tell me why we allow politicians after they've had hundreds of years to demonstrate their experience to solve problems in Congress to fall short of their responsibilities when it's needed?

Well, I'm tired of waiting for them to keep their promises, knowing some of their colleagues are trying to alter the Constitution from its original Doctrine to insight another Civil war. The question is, are we not concern about people in power who's not afraid of rendering no justice through their courts and in congress? It's important to ask ourselves what course of legal action can be taken to also change our corrupt Judicial system?

Especially, after we've known for years, Judges have taken unlawful advantage against our citizens ruining their lives, giving them a Felony sentence for minor crimes. Further, causing them to be rejected from the rest of this economic system for the rest of their lives, after they've paid their debt to society. Now we know judges and lawyers use their record of convictions to influence Americans to vote them in Congress, by targeting, Black Americans putting them in jail who've committed lesser crimes than the people we've voted for in Congress?

The system uses their criminal record to deny them good paying jobs through our unemployment system. Sure, we know it show's biases when the system refuses to give politicians felony records when they commit crimes that's never solved. (Why), We know their ball point pen could be more dangerous than a gun if it's not used properly. By not signing documents agreeing to help Millions of Americans live through wars/violence and the Virus! Obviously, they have the Audacity to open the door allowing Donald to run again for the presidency. When we know it wouldn't be tolerated if the candidate was of a different Ethnic background.

That's what causing fear of being removed from the political system because of violating their oath, degrading your vote. Targeting Black people trying to prevent them from leading us in the future. Nevertheless, politicians know people of color have gotten the death sentence for killing White men and women even when some of them were innocent of the crime. Now the rules have changed for those who hold the office of being (president)! You can't convict the president of any crime before he's term in office has expired. Even when he leaves office, it seems he'll still receive special treatment, preventing him from going to prison!

So, it's our job as Americans to get answers of why they refuse to exercise their Authority against him, knowing his term in office has expired. I wonder, who would've believed we would be fighting against (Autocracy) in the 21st Century? There's no excuse for this kind of negligence, unless White supremacist are recognized in congress as being honorable leaders turning to crime killing people?! Still, some of us sit back in our comfort zone from the pain and suffering that men women have endured on both-sides for telling the truth.

Please remember, if they can't admit this is a racist Country especially when it was built on (racism), then we've chosen the wrong politicians to lead us? Let's not forget, Native American who were also Black suffered the anguish as part of their legacy of foul play. Still, their conscience didn't change their aggression to inflect harm, by warring against them with guns being focused to take their land!! I know you've heard and read about them without thinking about the devastation it caused people who are different from the White population in this Country.

Obviously, this system of government refuses to teach what they've done to people in their schools here and worldwide. Preventing, their children growing up from experiencing a positive opinion about people who've suffered, yet we trust the same politicians to be fair politically?!! Now, for some politicians who've shown ethics and principles seems to have no place in politics anymore!! However, I guess it's hard to put all the blame on politicians because Americans should've known for centuries, we the people have chosen leaders whose motives were only focused on gaining power and wealth.

However, instead of picking our own leaders aside of politics to vote for, yes, we should've had enough foresight to see the inevitable. The reason these Palms are elected to Congress and for the presidency, it's not because their qualified to serve the American people. These politicians knew their opponents wouldn't have the financial support to compete with them on the world stage. Even now we've seen how frustrating it is for some Americans to be led by different Ethnic groups of people! Finally, we know those who've had the guts to say yes will be criticized profusely through the Media, especially by Fox News. Claiming those who speaks the truth about them, they're also accused of unethical acts!!

Yes, I'm aware these comments will be a challenge to reach the masses of people because of the narratives in this book. It's obvious these Southerners in those battle ground states would prefer a White man as a dictator instead of a diverse Democratic System, to choose someone different who understand how to lead from a pragmatic point of view! If they refuse to comply it would eliminate all chances of a diverse Congress to cast your Vote. If Americans allow this change of absolute power to

White supremacist, then all the years we've fought and died during the civil War and other Wars to be free was for naught.

However, if you're going to complain now, whining about reading the history of Americans deeds and actions against other people? Then my efforts to tell the truth won't matter to those who have no conscience of who's right or wrong, when someone is being killed unjustly. I'm writing about these crimes perpetrated against all Americans who believe in our Democratic system. They know they have the advantage, placing me in the opinions of the majority of Americans to judge my intent for giving my readers a history lesson! I know those Americans whose paying attention understand how difficult it is to be recognized globally.

Especially when some Authors are unknown to the public to voice their opinion about what's being tolerated in this country. Further, to be able to gain recognition of those in power to act favorably on these narratives, that really deserves their attention. Yes, I know if I gave praise to politicians for doing absolutely nothing to demonstrate their qualification to help people in need, then the general public might have a chance to read this book?!!

However, when you think about it, there's no doubt it's Mr. Donald J Trump's legacy they're trying to protect, knowing it had Catastrophic effect of our way of life. Nevertheless, I feel overwhelmed when I think about my ancestors and others being disappointed. Sweating sheading their blood, giving their life, fighting for a cause greater than themselves. Yes, I know it was heart breaking for American that's tired of listening to the same rhetoric every election cycle. Now we're listening to TV reporters saying a lot of Americans, care more about the economy, then losing their Constitutional rights and other privileges Americans are intitle to that's already mentioned in this book.

However, a lot of Americans are influenced by the same negative attitude their ancestors had, who once Hung Black people on tree limbs. Yelling derogatory statements while they were gasping for breath pleading for their life. Praying, for their (White Master Jesus) to deliver them from the hands of their oppressors, unfortunately for them that didn't happen! I admit I'm happy to expose the truth, and say what I know about our struggle through the mainstream Media and in Books. Hopefully, once they acknowledge the truth teaching what they've done to Black people in our schools. I know it will shade new light in concept about Black people and other Ethnic groups to understand the difference in opportunity between them growing into adulthood?

It's like a movie I saw years ago when someone said referring to White people (it's all in the breeding). Trying to insinuate Black people and their heritage aren't of good quality. Sure, they're going to allow White immigrants to come here from different countries because they say birds of a feather folk together. Now considering all the negative things they've done to people, it's hard for me to understand why they killed one of their comrades years ago in Germany? The man in question is (Adolf, Hitler). His legacy of hate for different Ethnic groups of people still lives in the minds and hearts of some Americans today. Now some politicians are helping to influence more people to join their organizations.

Whose goal is to have control of darker skinned people, by disrespecting or killing anyone who have a different opinion about how they should be treated!! Let's not forget, there was a time when Black soldiers also helped the Jew's in their war experiences. When they were fighting and defeating the Germans who also treated them with discrimination. It's a shame we don't have Millions of them standing with Black men and women after they went overseas fighting and dying, to win a war helping them to annihilate their menaced to the world.

Which makes me wonder where are the Jews now and other Ethnic groups of people in different countries, rendering their support by sub-plying them with nuclear weapons to defend their-self, when their existence is being threaten? Why aren't they here in solidarity expressing their contempt in the way Black people are being killed? Also standing with them while they're going through this ordeal struggling to survive with no protection from the judicial system. So White supremacist can feel safe preventing Black people from walking, driving through, or living in their communities?

Finally, people are realizing there are thousands if not millions of Hitler's followers and admirers who are disguising themselves here as American patriots? What a tragedy to live through this scene of hypocrisy, seeing thousands of Black men, women and others fighting to win this fight against this evil mentality! Now it appears the Jews and other White immigrants are shown more respect living in this Country than the descendance of Black people who were the Architect's building the country they value so much!! I think it's unconscionable how Black Americans efforts aren't valued for services rendered.

Further, to receive the financial and political backing and proper recognition they deserve as American citizens. Granting (African Americans Day) on May 3rd every year would be one way of showing their support, after so many years of neglect! Don't forget, Black men and women have celebrated the birthdays of presidents out of respect who've owned slaves, including Gorge Washington and Abraham Lincoln and 10 other presidents with the same resume of owning slaves. Still our history will show they are the last to be treated as Americans and the last to go to War against them, for reasons we all know would be justifiable!!

We know it's a fact, there's no other race of people in the world would tolerate this kind of abuse for 400 years without going to war if necessary to save their humanity. Now, let's talk about what are the rules when boundaries are crossed, and force is used against people for it to be justified judiciously for them to act violently to kill in self-defense, in response of being attacked?!! I wonder how long will Black Americans continue living in this mystical world of self-righteous behavior refusing to kill in self-defense when they're families are being murdered in their sleep?

What's so frustrating and moving for me, is when the people of the world allow White people to challenge the way God created mankind by trying to eliminate them entirely from this planet. I guess it's out of envy because they know Black men and women's history goes further back in time, to educate people about the first human-beings God created on Earth. Still, it doesn't matter because what politicians are trying to hide won't change the (facts). Now they're showing fear, because Americans are tired of listening to their rhetoric when it's not helping them grow as a Nation!!

CHAPTER 5

Why can't we say it loud and clear what we really feel about them to the world, so our future together will be void of those racial comments? Further, acknowledging to ourselves we've allowed these barriers to exist between us too long, preventing our growth as Human-beings our children would be proud of. Sure, it's their prerogative if some Americans want to be submissive and die without holding someone accountable for the deaths of their loved-ones. However, I will not forget what Donald is trying to accomplish by using old tactics to divide us!!

Even when the Devils of hate that still exist within the soul of this Country are constantly rebelling against them, which leaves Americans powerless to improve their abhorrent conditions? History will not be passive telling the truth to our great grandchildren in their history books. Making them aware how this generation of republicans contributed to the genocide of their ancestors. It's a fact if any of our adversaries would've caused this kind of grief with Millions of lives lost in this country, war would've been inevitable. It's obvious the reason we're not at war it's because this tragedy happened within the perimeter of our safety zone, caused by the majority of men and women in Congress.

Let's talk about the Electoral college system of voting that elected Donald Trump. Now people are asking why they are risking their lives during the Corona-virus epidemic? When those southern states seem to dominate the final results by preventing the majority vote, to be the deciding factor of who wins or loses. Unfortunately, after 400 plus years we're still waiting for an explanation of the agreement they made between general Lee and general Grant. Allowing these Southern States so much power after the civil war ended in 1865? I wonder is this all a conspiracy to deceive those who's constantly acting naïve hoping, for the impossible to happen in this generation giving, Black people equal justice under the law?!!

Well, to those who haven't seen much change in the way they've been treated in those Southern States, what's your opinion about the electoral college system of Voting now? If the majority system of voting was in-effect this tragedy wouldn't have happened. Like it or not it seems nothing Americans can do to correct these mistakes when we're giving power to White men's rule of governing instead of the people's rule. The question is when will we be willing to do what's necessary to change what these republicans are legislating in our Courts? Further, I know once the majority of Americans become familiar with a new way of governing which allows more diversity in our leaders. They need a chance to demonstrate their ability to make positive changes in the House and the Senate in congress!!

Then Americans will have more confidence in the system, with different Ethnic groups as leaders. I believe that mixture of ideas, would produce positive decisions that every American can benefit from. That will change this Atmosphere of grief living in a nonproductive society that's always causing division among us. Yeah, it's sad and I admit Black people are only acknowledged as Americans in times of war. Giving, them the freedom to fight for their Country, but not the freedom to choose who should lead them through a crisis that's taking us back in time? Now I feel proud, to write about those handful of freedom fighters past and present, including (Minister, Louis Farrakhan). Soldiering for the people, which it seems anyone with morals and principles are being Exiled from the public. It's my honor to acknowledge him and those leaders who fought hard against the odds to end corruption in this country, I would like to say (Thank you Sir, for your service)!!

I predict your names will have permanent favor in the minds of the oppressed in our history books for generations to come! Really, without your service challenging this issue of race which threatens your lives, including the late Mr. Malcom X. He also showed determination to fight against Autocracy, and any form of racism until he was assassinated. Yet without fear Mr. Malcom X, and others were determined to get their message of unity to all American regardless of the colors of their skin. There aren't enough words in my vocabulary that's worthy of the gratitude for the work you and your constituents Black and (Palms), describing lighter, not (White) have done.

To create a world free of conflict that will enhance a feeling of being united especially among Black people in this battle fighting for equality. So, every American can live here at peace with there-self and with the world!! Yes, we know some Americans at some points have participated in things they regret and ashamed to admit in public. Do you remember the (Tea Party)? If not let me tell you, Americans should be a shame that we're not advocating when the first Black President Mr. Obama was in office. The Tea Party and some Republicans, men and women had a lot of negative things to say about him without fearing any retribution from their colleagues for disrespecting him in public.

I guess politicians didn't realize it mattered to Americans how disrespectful and insensitive their claims were, that was unsubstantiated. Saying that he lied while he was speaking to Americans, trying to inform them about his daily activities. Since then, we've experienced such a tragedy during the Trump era, now you can hear a pin drop on a rug. From the silence of the Tea party being reluctant to be visual and voice their opinion about the negative things Mr. Trump was doing while in office. However, instead of them being willing to talk about Mr. Trump, and what he said in a disgraceful way about our first Black president, it showed a sense of envy or jealousy to refer to Mr. Obama in that manor?!

Have you noticed, now they hide like cowards afraid of being exposed to answer questions about these issues of treason, being advocated by Republicans in our political system. Now politicians are making excuses about what Mr. Trump has done trying to confuse the public. However, I wouldn't be surprised if the Tea party played a major part keeping the republicans silent about Mr. Trump Ethnic background. So, with all of the complaints about Donald Trump, members of the Tea party seem to have a problem, accusing him of Millions of Americans dying during his watch in office! (Yes, I wrote it), because if it was Mr. Obama responsible for millions of Americans dying, they would've asked for the death penalty!

Finally, Black people realize they're only servants to a system that's rejecting them as being creatable citizens when trying to express their right to vote. Unfortunately, you would think after centuries of the same treatment Americans would believe Black people when they say they're tired of being abused by the system? You can be assured, if Americans continue to follow Mr. Trump's clan to violate us as Americans, then nothing will change in the house or the Senate.

Furthermore, this isn't a mistake calling what they're doing unfortunate, when they continue to exemplify what most Americans have tried to avoid being called (Corrupt). It's obvious they have no shame dealing with public opinion about they're decision to be loyal to Donald Trump, regardless of what he's done to deceive Americans and their way of life. Nevertheless, this is the first time in years we're able to talk and write about these tragedies openly to the public! Although, it's not reported that Black people support these police officers with

Millions of dollars hoping they're keep them safe, but their reward is being killed unarmed at home in their pajamas!

Now you can bet, Americans can't make excuses claiming they didn't know about the violence these people have to deal with every-day. Even now politicians' strategy is threatening people to be silent, and nonvolant about the same issues that kept our ancestors' bond by slavery. Unfortunately, so far when they voice their opinions, which is the only weapon they have to protect their-self especially from the Government and against violence from police officers. For centuries politicians have stalled on duty to serve and protect whomever are the victims of crimes in some States that would invoke the death penalty.

It's unconscionable, the way Black people were deceived thinking, if they showed their patriotism being willing to fight and die in wars against their enemies and obey their constitutional laws. This Country would treat them fairly with more respect than immigrant that killed Black and White soldiers in their countries years ago in Germany, and in other parts of the world.

Now they're forgetting who they've fought wars with, and won against some of these White immigrants who's now considered to be Americans!!

Nevertheless, it shows in the faces of Black people who continue to be rejected from the lack of change in their lives. To accept these people as Americans who killed some of their comrades in battle years ago!! Well, if you listen hard enough, you'll hear conversations are different among its devoted servants, asking why should they continue serving this unjust system? Or stop believing in their Jewish god who've allowed without pity these unspeakable abhorrent conditions to continue against them?

While serving their god with faith and devotion, hoping to be delivered from White oppression and tyranny every-day. It seems Justice is trapped in the shadows of time waiting to be discovered for anyone who have the courage and fortitude to risk their lives to Harness it? Now they are asking should they create their own God instead of a Jewish god, who would be more sympathetic to their cause? Although we allow our children to attend their schools to be educated by the system of their political will, to serve as part of their duty as Americans.

It's unfortunate after cooperating with their system and the issues they're having with politicians. Who, haven't changed their demands on them to be nonviolent, when their sons and daughters are being murdered in the streets. Still their sons and daughters continue to serve in Uniform fighting in their armed forces. Now, in spite of their loyalty, politicians still ignore their patriotism, without mentioning them on the News as first responders in life and death situations. Now, their comrades in war aren't concerned if Black people are ignored being considered for executive positions, even though they're qualified for the job once they come back from fighting wars.

Once they're recommended for the job, they ignore their qualifications to work in different categories especially in sports. Nevertheless, those who are hired, when they're successful in their careers they must endure resentment. Especially, from the White population because now they're living in middle class communities around their adversaries' White sons and daughters. That's why they're obviously trying to avoid contact with them publicly and privately. Tell me, why should that matter if this isn't a racist Country? Unfortunately, it's obvious Palms feelings of hate and separation is passed down to their children from generations to Centuries.

It's all part of a strategy, to remind their children that's part of their (legacy) to reject Black people from living in their communities, because they're different. Yes, it makes me feel proud that didn't define Black people as a nation of strength and stability including the word (Nigga), didn't degrade the character of who they are as a Nation. It's amazing how that disrespectful word (Nigga), is being used now as slang for laughter, to identify them individually. Nevertheless, even with the name calling they took pride in displaying fortitude to survive against the odds.

Now I'm sending a message in this book that our job isn't finished until racism is no longer part of our society. Unfortunately, if we fail in this effort then the next generation won't escape these pitfalls of those 3 subjects I've mentioned in this book. Unless Americans have the guts to change this antiquated way of thinking. For those who aren't paying attention, try to remember, if these abhorrent conditions and their negative attitudes toward people don't change, it will eventually cause chaos in the world! Simply because we were incapable like our ancestors to solve this problem ourselves without using violence.

It's time Americans know, to commit an immoral act against each other, should be considered as transgression against divine law. Nevertheless, if those components of being evil is part of our humanity at birth, it could also be part of our DNA? Seriously if those words are true, that condition may prevent some humans from being spiritually Holy in this life and in death. Now the question is why were we created by God to start from the beginning of our existence here on Earth. I wonder, could it be a test of endurance, or a test of how we show our humanity toward each other in this life? Further testing us from knowing absolutely nothing about this life, and without having any memory if we existed physically or spiritually in another form of existence before entering this body?

I've heard anything is possible, which I wonder, did that world exist somewhere within the Utopia of God's mind, revealing a world that wasn't ruled by men but of gods. Who mastered showing compassion toward each other as an example to follow before we entered our mother's womb? Sure, it's hard to understand this lesson of survival, by the time our brain absorbs it physically spiritually and politically here. It leaves us confused trying to choose with some accuracy and concern which one is the right path to follow? Or have faith God will intervene, showing everybody the right choices to make? Now they know the struggle to achieve success wasn't easy through books because at one time they weren't available to the majority of indigent Black people because of slavery.

Nevertheless, I believe when they weren't able to read or write for hundreds of years, should've been taken under consideration. Why, because some of them still believe in fantasies after being denied their right to be Educated. Therefore, that lack of education seemed to have caused a lot of division between the people they love and others, trying to distinguish the difference in truth/falsehoods and fantasies. For years Black people have concentrated on learning those two diabolical subjects most of their adult lives. It has left them totally dependent on this system to determine which direction they're headed, forward or backward?

However, politicians are making it harder for them to solve other problems, that plagues their total existence! Which keeps politicians in total control if they succeed or fail. Especially, in a system that's designed by politicians to mislead them politically, spiritually and economically. That's why there are fewer Black, and White (Millionaires) today! Unfortunately for them, I've concluded in my studies why some people resist the truth in this generation. That's why, it doesn't attract the kind of interest a lot of Americans are willing to accept. (Why)?

For years we haven't talked about how some politicians are consistent trying to destroy our humanity, especially if we're convinced by them to be dishonest and deceitful toward each other. Which causes more tension between us, for purposes that should be beneath our character and social experiences, to communicate with each other in a prudent way. Somehow, we've lost that moral substance that was attached to the principles we've tried to live by. Especially when it was held in our grasp that generated respect from other world leaders! My problem is after this experience living in a modern world of deceit, what will the educational system teach our children next?

Especially, when they've seen corruption being manifested in our social and political gatherings? Just imagine if morals and principles are no longer part of our Ethnic code for restoring stability among future generations of our children? If we relinquish that effort what courses of study would be adequate in their curriculum, that would measure up to our standards of showing human dignity to the world they can respect?!! This political system makes me wonder if Americans was hit so hard, they've been blind sighted by Donald Trump and his clan to know the difference between right and wrong?

Is this a new definition for the word Patriots when a group of misinformed people started rebelling against the procedures of their own country? Really, it's shameful, what politicians are offering is beneath the character most Americans have chosen to live by!! I wonder, who are these people other than

Donald Trump that's acting above the law, causing some reporters refusal to expose them to the public? I thought when you lose a war, you're not entitle to have the kind of power to dictate voting privileges in that state, especially when your ancestors were considered as traders to the Union? Now their storming the Capital holding the Confederate Flag threatening to kill other patriots who abide by the constitution?

It's unfortunate, we don't know the names of politicians who negotiated the terms between the North and South, that grants traitors and their supporter's the right to prevent people from Voting, now and in the future?! It appears after they lost the war, they refused to alleviate racism in those southern states. Furthermore, who would believe, they're still showing their contempt after their performance at the Capital. Please don't forget Mr. John Lewis the Congressman that fought against racism most of his adult life?

This is what he said before he died and I'm paraphrasing, "when you see injustice say something and get in the way on Election Day." Well guys after the Republicans were mad at Ms. Hilary Clinton, they spent Millions of dollars trying to dishonor her for getting rid of her emails. While, accusing her of 3 Americans death in Benghazi claiming it was a devastating act of cruelty and negligence. Unfortunately, the voters believed that rhetoric and were convinced Ms. Clinton couldn't be trusted. Now Republicans are undecided and debating if Mr. Trump should be held accountable for the deaths he may or may not have caused by not following the advice of doctors and scientist!! It's no secret even now the Republicans are still without shame to be governed by this kind of a man, who shows no interest in keeping his oath to his followers!!

CHAPTER 6

Will God forgive them For This?

There's no excuse for Americans allowing Donald Trump's cowardice behavior and his influence to take route among the republican party, who sold their souls to Lucifer in the flesh (Donald Trump). Now this ex-president, seemed to have turned our citizens into sacrificial lambs with the Corona-virus, trying to secure his leadership position for another term in office. This type of neglect was unprecedented and deadly, especially when Hospitals refused to accept patients, knowing their citizens couldn't survive without treatment!! Please remember if politicians are still allowing the judicial system to shield those responsible for the deaths of Americans.

Then all the principles we teach our children are worthless, unless we clean house by having an equal amount of diversity of colorful people in Congress. Also in the judicial system, to further represent the different legal issues that determines the fate of all

Americans lives not just a few. Still my ancestors are repeating in my mind, if Americans are not led by ethics to speak out against racism every-day until these massacres stop. Then they should reevaluate the content of what they represent to the world. So, if people's massages of faith do not make a difference regardless of what books they're reading or advocating.

Justice will not be implemented as part of what they believe world-wide. Causing their opinions to have a devastating effect between life and death fighting in this world for their right to live. Hoping, all Americans won't be denied a democratic way of expressing their views when they vote. Please remember, this subject isn't something we should ignore, after years of fighting against this storm of rage that continues every day to push our effort back. I know once we've had that dilemma under control by fighting, we're be rewarded in ways we haven't seen before. Let's make a mental decision, to be prepared to stop this way of living by bigotry and violence, by having a growing appetite for peace to exist within the boundaries of the soul of America)?!

There's no other way to solve this problem if we don't commune and admit to ourselves no one is above the law. Or built this Country without help from different Ethnic groups of people who fought and died for the same cause. Sure, we know I'll biggest problem is convincing politicians to share the benefits of war equally among the American people. Yes, I know we've talked about this issue for centuries, even now we have to tolerate these acts of neglect that's deliberately forced on us in different ways. Only because Americans allowed a majority of White men to rule in Congress, who don't give a damn about their patriotic duties to solve our problems.

However, it would be to our advantage if we stop ignoring, they're not interested in sharing anything of value with the American people. Or willing to be responsible for not preventing the negative way they've treated their fellow Americans. Some people are unaware, of unknown Author's like me are solely depended on social media if things don't change to advertise our books to the public. So, it's unfortunate the mainstream media make it difficult for new Authors to be recognized without Millions of sales of their books. Knowing that would be almost impossible to achieve without Radio, or TV advertisement.

Nevertheless, there's so many unanswered questions about why we lie to ourselves and others about the advantages White Authors have through the mainstream media. Which in most cases unknown

Authors are restricted, because they're not backed by Millionaires financially to advertise their books to the public? Especially if you're writing about corruption in our political system. However, if by chance I can stop people from teaching these same lies to our children about Black people. Which we've allowed their teachings to be a disaster for them trying to learn.

Further, to understand what it means to believe the fantasies we teach our children at an early age. Not knowing the devastating effect, it will have when they become adults. Especially after they were influenced by them to believe life after death will be a realistic experience. Which I know life only exist through our DNA in our children and grand-children)? Furthermore, I can't understand why it's still a mystery shaking off why Americans Black and White continue to believe a philosophy someone wrote 2,000 or more years ago about Jesus, knowing his true identity has been hidden from the public?

What's so baffling, is most Christians believe when you have faith it automatically transforms their beliefs into reality. If by chance those people did exist, stop showing different images of them in photos, and paintings?!! Critics have said the Bible I'm writing about now has changed Millions of people's lives who read it, some for the better some for the worse. The Bible has also separated families and friends from each other over some imaginary doctrine written in a book based on their faith and belief in a Jewish God. Whose narratives are without a realistic version of what they believed really happened.

Now I've come to the conclusion I can't blame King James, who's the Author of the English translated version of the Bible, for the way people think or who they choose to believe or have faith in. The Bible was supposed to represent a Godly way to worship that was different from other religious theories. I wouldn't be surprised if the Bible was written hundreds of years before it was introduced to Americans on July 4,1776, and turned out to be one of the bestselling book in history! Even now while I'm writing, people of different ethnic backgrounds are fascinated by the doctrine written in that book.

However, it's unbelievable, how they seem to be intrigued with Jews everyday struggles about their shepherds watching over their sheep. Teaching us, about their battles of life and death, fought and won by their King's and Queen's against other Ethnic groups of people, using a strategy to kill with their god's blessings. The truth is the last thing I want to give the impression, that I'm a righteous man writing about the Bible, (I'm not). I do believe people are advocating unrealistic manuscripts using God's name as a reference of approval? All I'm saying is, I hope no logical thinking person will deny where we're going when our body dies, and that's in the ground.

Unfortunately, I was told speaking with family and friends. If I want my book to reach the public don't write negative things about the Bible. It's, because Christians keep relating to the Bible as God's word. My responsibility as a truth teller, is to write and speak about what some people fear and that's exposing lies to the misinformed. So, they won't follow the same pattern believing manuscripts that's (tearing us apart mentally). These realities they hide in the shadows of unspoken words to the public, and it's still waiting to be discovered by anyone who have the guts to acknowledge truth, regardless of the person who wrote it.

Moreover, the problem we're facing now, is when people believe something they were taught all their lives. It creates challenges making it harder for them to accept a different philosophy they haven't heard before. It's unfortunate, some people don't understand, some things you believe is not necessarily true!! I know we've always had problems believing someone we don't know. However, I don't expect people to be brave enough to accept my opinion about what I know are facts simply because I wrote it. I know it's hard making tough decisions over night based on if I'm right or wrong about life after death or any other subjects that's written in this book. Especially, until they've had a chance to research it for their-selves? I know this is a generational teaching that continues to be taught regardless of the mental damage it may inflict in the mind of the believer.

However, as adults, our children are depending on their parents to be thinking prudently about their future, to know certain facts that wasn't revealed to their parents and to them as a child!! I personally know it's impossible to show any response about anything while you're physically buried under 6 feet of dirt. Or from your ashes being contained in a vase while you're waiting to be called back into existence from an unknown source of power?! Now we should ask why it's so important for White men to change Black people's way of thinking from their African heritage.

Invading their identity their Language and the Gods they believed in for thousands of years prior to Christianity? Christians are saying you must believe and have faith in a new Jewish god they serve with the Holy Ghost as part of its attributes.

In which, it's similar to another fictional character (Superman), who was faster than a speeding Bullet and more powerful than a locomotive. However, I might not live long enough to witness the recovery of the mental state of my people, not being willing to accept facts from fiction about this issue. I know when their eyes finally open to the truth it will be obviously clear it's a difference between the two that seems to keep us so confused.

Hopefully before they experience death they will control their mental state, allowing them to pass their knowledge to the next generation of their children! It shouldn't be hard to understand they've constructed their religion into flourishing (business) collecting a substantial amount of revenue! Please believe me if you only help people because you were inspired by God, instead of doing it because it was the noble or humane thing to do. Then you need a fresh course of what being civilized really means? Furthermore, no one should be listening if people are trying to prove this doctrine of faith and belief has any relevance to reality.

Sure, some Christians sing and speak in a compelling way to influence you to join their organization. However, can we recover from hundreds of years of brainwashing to engage in a realistic stance for truth? Further, knowing about the facts of life, it also took a while before I realized knowing or hearing the truth doesn't necessarily make you want to shout for (joy), when all your life you were taught something totally different! There was a statement in the Bible, know the truth and it shall set you (free)!! The problem is at that time, I wasn't prepared for the devastated consequences of knowing the truth. In which may cause anger or (death) to those who advocate it.

Sometimes I face a lot of resentment among family and friends, and others who act afraid of living a lie for centuries without knowing they've been used for monetary value. I realize it's not easy to gain trust from some people when I expose their faith and belief to realistic facts. One more thing I know, the begotten son of my God never existed on this planet as a White man. Still these religious dynasties show a White man's face of Jesus to be Authentic, sometime Blonde, or Brunet? Further, these statistics about him was not substantiated by facts.

I employ you to consider, if you've ever seen a White man with hair like lamb's wool and feet like polished brass? However, knowing the truth has caused a lot of wars with people here and in different countries, because all of them want their god to look like them, which in my view is impossible.

Why, because the Supreme being isn't Human, it's obvious if he was Human, He couldn't have physical presents everywhere at the same time. Moreover, you can believe this subject about going to Heaven carries the same weight that's too frustrating for some critics to accept.

Unfortunately, all we know now from scientist and Astronauts report about the different galaxy's, their studies prove its field with gasses. However, a lot of us are prone to violence when we hear the truth, especially from someone we don't like. Well according to their Bible Jesus also wasn't liked by all the people he tried to help!! So, I would like to dedicate this book to my children and grandchildren, who may be willing to sacrifice their lives and popularity to expose this system that's controlling our minds living in a world filled with uncertainties, also believing in equal justice under their laws.

It's important to know what it means to tell the truth when masses of people are ready to explode about this issue, because a lot of people have lived in the dark too long, accepting what's written in books to be truthful for centuries. Moreover, if my people want to learn about this daring attempt to set the record straight, they only have two choices. Either prioritize facts from fiction or continue to live in a world filled with unsubstantiated ideas to be realistically true. By influencing us to (believe) something exist we can't see, instead of being taught what we know exists by having some physical evidence to prove it. There's always' another option, they can turn on the light of reason which will make a positive difference in their decisions about life and its fantasies!

Or is it possible we're all waiting to Mature about this issue, or is it our passion to refuse to grow up mentally believing something we were told about Jesus, instead of accepting what we know about him according to history? It seems we'd rather follow a tradition, to engage in different kinds of religious doctrines. Switching from one denomination to the next still searching for the truth? Instead of what we know could be real to celebrates, (African Americans Day). In which would be something gratifying for all of us to look forward to while we live!

Who knows with the racial problems we're having now I guess it won't happen Nationally unless Americans demands it? Nothing frustrates me more than the hypocrisy of some Palms who will smile in your face claiming to be Christians one moment, and won't hesitate to kill you within a blink of an eye the next. Just because you're different culturally ethnically and morally! It's, because of this misunderstanding we have of the human race with the illusion some Americans believe they're superior to their Black ancestors? However, it's time to ask why, have we addressed ourselves as human-beings when at times we act more like animals, in which this analysis of violence seems similar between the two Animals to kill?

One kills for survival, and the other kill for power at the Capital on Jan 6? I guess the cliché about one bad apple in a barrel spoiling the rest seems to be true. Moreover, you can bet without a doubt it's harder to be separated from the ones we love who's trying to destroy us as a Nation!! I need your support to acknowledge their suffering and fortitude which produced the energy from which I write these humble words of hope for those Black Americans who's still being persecuted by some reporters and our elected officials! It's no doubt just writing about our problems may not change any-thing. If we allow our negative instincts to domi-nate what's needed for us to succeed as a Nation.

For many years we've avoided discussing these 3 subjects I've mentioned in this book, because it seems to be unpopular. To write or speak to those who refuse to teach Black history in their schools because what they've done is too horrible to put in words literally! It's astonishing how those 3 negative subjects have affected and destroyed in some cases the hopes and dreams of people's lives. Further, by holding animosity against each other because of our differences of opinions about those subjects.

Through the years I've heard people saying it's time for Americans to rationalize why we continue to accept the negative behavior of politicians who create Sedition in the minds of Americans during their term in office. With all due respect I wonder, is it the food we eat or the water we drink that allows us to ignore their misuse of power and influences that comes with the position of being in congress?

Furthermore, it's amazing how politicians continue to use their books to control our future here. Telling Americans how far they can go on this planet and even in death, (Heaven or Hell)?! I wonder if that's another fictional bed time story to scare us, or is it a proven fact we can substantiate traveling through time? Leaving our bodies after death traveling upward from the grave toward the Heavens to another world? Although this mystery has yet to be solved, or proven to be a fact, it's better to find out the truth for yourself. Instead of believing some fictional characters some scholars wrote about a Jewish god in a book.

However, it's amazing how Christians put themselves on a high pedestal, thinking they are that advanced intellectually to determine where we're going after death. Further, telling us to accept the King James Version of the Bible as an absolute fact, to be the only pathway to happiness in life and in death? So, while we're waiting to reach this mystical world, we have problems here in this Country to deal with. For example, trying to protect ourselves dodging rubber bullets and teargas, while trying to exist here with some dignity. Nevertheless, we're still trying to show respect for our-selves and police officers who's trying to kill us!!

We should be focusing on the dangers ahead, because the rules have changed, politicians are showing favoritism allowing White people to pro-test with guns, without being killed if they show aggression. So far, the written messages I've seen or heard concerning Black peoples struggle with police violence, is mostly spoken from local Ministers here and there in different cities!

CHAPTER 7

When devotion is needed

Obviously, it's not to politicians' advantage to be fair, from the length of time black people struggled in this Country, their complaints should've been taken seriously! Now, if politicians and reporters' attitude toward Black people don't change. Their children won't have the satisfaction to show pride of their own race, especially while their mentors are alive trying desperately to make their lives better in the future. I've concluded those predators who's trying to prevent their progress should be exposed to the public, so we're know who to blame in Court when it's their time to face the masses of people whose lives they've destroyed.

Yes, I wrote it again because it's important to keep repeating this issue until the killings stops. Sure, we've known for years, White jurors in court are not considering the facts being Black, always helped to contribute to their fate, of either death or imprisonment! Still, we know, it didn't require multiple bullets in their bodies to subdue them after they fell dead and unarmed. Seldomly it's written in books, the reason they filled their bodies with multiple bullets, it's to eliminate all witnesses to the crimes against our citizens.

Unfortunately, we've yet convicted stand your ground killers in these southern states, their officials make excuses why no one is charged with their deaths? This must be investigated; the reason White people aren't dying from the same police stops? Obviously being White they're not suspicious of committing a crime? It's a pattern when they're accused of murder, reporters keep saying, let's not rush to judgement when a lot of questions needs answers. Still, they refuse to write, or broadcast the unlawful acts police officers are engaged in, until their investigation of the crime is over?

Personally, I know if these White men weren't armed patrolling in their communities, this charade of killing Black people wouldn't be on the News. Thanks to Mr. Donald Trump we know the slang peace on earth and good will to all men, was just a cliché not a reality for Black people. This lesson should be taught in our schools, when you're devoted to ethics it sets a pathway to righteousness unless you deviate from it. It's obvious some of our ancestors strived to have that kind of righteous quality that seems to be part of my DNA, and others who's willing to follow that same pattern of conduct.

People are saying when someone kills a Black man, they're destroying the image of God roaming the Earth? If that's true it would really be a (dagger) in the heart of White supremacist. Yeah, it seems people are aware of some Americans moral standard is slipping away, because of their ego and interest to obtain power. However, now Mr. Trump has emerged as a racist, it's plain to see when you scatter the secrets of deceit, the (evidence) is there to see it for your-self. I wonder, have we decided now we were wrong about honesty being the best policy? Obviously, it's no doubt we're listening to the same psychology some politicians used to get away with murdering people in the 16th century.

Actually, I would be ashamed if we were that naive to believe the same rhetoric of them being innocent of crimes!! Furthermore, because of my age this may be my last time writing about this racial issue, because it's too frustrating, and I must admit I get upset voicing my opinion when it doesn't seem to matter one way or the other!! I hate to say critics thought there would be more support from the religious Dynasties to speak in Black people's defense. Just out of respect remembering those people of different Ethnic backgrounds supported them financially for centuries. Now their silence is deafening in support of them fighting against injustice.

Just check their records, the only religious groups who's speaking out against these shootings of Black people are Minister, Louis Farrakhan, Rev. Al, Sharpton, MLK the third, and Dr. William, Barber. Just to mention a few of their constituencies who are on the front-line every-day in defense of the American people. However, when White people also known as (Palms), are the majority being killed, they repeat a slogan we're familiar with saying. (We're all in this together) when it pertains mostly to their safety and inconveniences. Why are we waiting to declared racism a state of emergency in every State, until this problem is solved?

That's when all Americans of different Ethnic backgrounds come together to help fight against this problem like in times of War? Now people are asking where do we go from here, are we headed for disaster, or making the effort to solve this problem faster? I know when it's all said and done, we all have some good qualities that sometimes needs to be nurtured toward being a better Human-being. When that happens we hope all of us won't have a need to carry weapons to feel safe. It's obvious this paranoia people feel about Black people only begins when they leave their own Communities. So, if people aren't willing to take time to communicate with each other, I believe the animosity they feel now could get worst?

Now I've come to the conclusion these conditions Black people have endured even from the beginning of slavery weren't meant to be fully eradicated. It was designed only to give the illusion of hope for those who believed politicians would help solve their problems. So, looking back in time it's impossible for anyone to see change, which would be suitable to make a difference according to our standard now in the 21st Century. Thanks to a new age of freedom fighters, they might bring a different concept of who we are as Americans. Moreover, I believe whoever said those words (Birds of a feather flock together) should've extended it to Human-beings, if we don't change our concept of being separated!!

So far that's the way some people expressed the way they feel, except when they're in fox holes with Black men and women fighting against their enemies. Sharing a common bond eating rations together trying to defend their-self against bombs grenades and gun fire. However, once Black soldiers' men and women come back to their homes in America, then it becomes a color issue. That's why when Black people talk about (Black lives Matter), they hoped Palms would show the world how Black Soldiers die trying to protect their-self and Palm Soldiers in battle!!

Actually, I would love to write about something different, and I will if the killings of Black people stop! So, what's their alternatives if the old ways aren't sufficient with a majority of White politicians in Congress? Nevertheless, we can't continue voting for people who can't provide the kind of leadership that's needed. To grow our economy and bridge gaps passing over our conflicts with each other? Let's not sugarcoat these violent acts against Black people, and be honest about what they've tolerated for years without being violent. However, their value should also be evaluated from an economic point of view. Living in a society that prospers from unlimited amounts of wealth because of their talent in different fields of entertainment.

Plus, an additional trillion dollars which stems from them being competitive in sports and in other businesses in different categories. Unfortunately, it's not appreciated to help save their lives politically and judiciously through legislation. Yes, even though their ancestors worked hard in the fields every-day. Still, they were determined to survive under conditions that were unspeakably horrible just to please their masters. Oh, believe me politicians did succeed to rebuild a failed economy with a sizable amount of Revenue off the book's and on the backs of Black Americans.

Unfortunately, after they earned the money picking cotton with other chores that produced Millions if not Billions of dollars. Nevertheless, it's unconscionable now these politicians are saying they won't pass a bill. That will take them out of poverty regardless of the sacrifices they've made to serve this country! Black people will never forget the 40 acres of land and a mule (promised) and denied to their ancestors who fought in the civil war? I guess, they forgot the money they used didn't belong to politicians it belonged to their Ancestors for their labor!! Now, we have to share part of our income every year paying Taxes for services we're not receiving!

Politicians should consider people who have a history of families being slaves here, should be exempt from paying Taxes. Just out of respect, because their ancestors worked hundreds of years without pay. If not, how can politicians' example of justice be credible in the minds of people, who know what Justice looks and feels like! Even if politicians feared for their lives, it shouldn't stop their obligation to treat them fairly, which is supposed to be part of their duty as public servants.

Just giving a Holiday in their honor (African Americans Day), still isn't enough to ease the pain. Suffering for years, nevertheless it's a start in the right direction to show some empathy! If Politicians refuse to grant the Holliday, I fear future generations of black people will be protesting and this time using gun violence against racism for another 400 years if necessary. I repeat they're still feeling some pain looking at the difference, with White immigrants only having to pass a written test to have full benefits of being treated as Americans!

Nevertheless, what's puzzling answering the question is Justice still blind, when White people can contribute much-less in service? When Black people contributed that and more to earn full citizenship, which they have yet (received). Furthermore, I know if we succeed by taking the lead in this effort, I'm sure it would be motivating giving hope to other Black and Brown children here and in different countries around this Nation. So, the only way we can end this battle of inequality, I'm asking all my readers please, spread the word and let's make this Holiday Universal)!!

CHAPTER 8

The Killer

Man would that be something of interest and pride to extend down to the next generations of our children and grandchildren to celebrate everywhere? The reason I wrote this book, I felt a sense of pride when I thought about all of my grandchildren great-grand also great-great grandchildren yes, you're right I've seen most of them. They give me hope for the future, knowing they are the extinction of American's hopes and dreams, of having a better chance to succeed. Further, I know sharing the weight and responsibility of this effort is not an easy task to accomplish. Although this tragedy has lasted for hundreds of years prior to their birth, it probably will give courage to others to fulfill their destiny, by helping to stop the violence, through their love and support for this movement.

I know it will not only be dangerous for them on this tedious journey to maintain the courage to continue fighting. Trying to end this particular type of cruelty against humanity punishing them by death, for the way God created them Black. The question is how long will they be motivated to carry this battle across the finish line. Especially if Americans who believe in this fight are distracted by other disasters, delaying their efforts to win this kind of war? I guess the only comfort for me trying to solve this problem, is hoping this book will inspire our youth to fight on regardless of how long it takes!! One reason I continue pleading to the American people for their support is because now we have the power to change our own destiny.

From being frustrated by not having access to a positive movement that will inspire people to participate in this fight on every level if necessary. The only way to achieve success all Americans must have the same passion to fight and win regardless of the opposition. They should recognize they've been taken for a ride too long in the opposite direction of being successful. Waiting for more deaths to occur against their own people, coupled with other tragedies for accepting this kind of aggression, to continue politically and economically against them.

Now, it appears we haven't learned from the civility we've used in the past, giving them more power through our vote that hasn't changed for 400 years. Yes, at my age I've wondered what will they try next to hinder people from succeeding once they've been targeted to fail like me? Tragically, now they're speaking bolder individually saying what their objectives are which is contrary to everything we've fought and died for. I guarantee, you can be assured this effort to remove these southern politicians from office is not going to be easy, because they're armed with guns, and they have influence in our courts to rule in their favor!

I employ we only have 2 alternatives, 1 keep the system we have now with a majority of men and women whose legislations have kept us divided for hundreds of years. Or 2 get ready for war, because these racist politicians are not going to change, their views about Black people or White supremacy. If we succeed defeating them in war, either from our deaths or the deaths of others to accomplish a goal of having equal opportunity! Hopefully the value of that endeavor would be priceless to invoke again the majority rule in voting; instead of giving these minority southern states special treatment through our electoral system of voting.

Or we can continue to support the Tea party with their version of hate. The same ones who were very visible with their likes and dislikes during Mr. Obama's presidency. Now they're hiding in the shadows spreading the same disease through politicians, focusing their dislikes toward minorities!! So far, under these terrible conditions, I can only hope Americans can understand what I'm trying to accomplish. Hopefully, by echoing the lost words of those Americans Black and White who weren't documented for their services in our history books.

It would be unpatriotic, if we forget those patriots who feared for their lives, if they didn't keep their mouths shut, to expose politicians who showed no responsibility keeping their oath to the Constitution. Now they're trying to stop women's right to choose Abortion in those Southern states. That's another subject I will discuss later in this book!! Furthermore, how long will we ignore those southern states that's always been a thorn in the side of our progress for hundreds of years? Sometimes it's frustrating trying to convince people to face facts about judges who's delaying the public from receiving justice.

Unfortunately, being a citizen of this country Black people will always be reminded about their ancestors being hung on those southern trees, pleading for their lives!! However, we know a lot of Americans benefited from their suffering, living in luxury homes while Black people continue their lives with bowed heads thanking God just to be live. Even in the 21st century they continue to suffer, instead of singing Victory songs about the positive changes in their lives. Once we admit to ourselves it's our fault if Americans of different Ethnic backgrounds always reframe from discussing those 3 subjects written in this book.

However, it could be our lack of duty toward each other, failing to fight and die if necessary for the same principle's our ancestors sacrificed their lives to uphold. Unfortunately, it seems that's the only way politicians will understand our message of life or death in a compelling way. There's an old saying, if you want something on this level that's not worth dying for, it isn't worth having. Now, the opportunity is in our grasp to use a different approach. Letting future generations of our children know those are the 3 subject's we've been battling to change our future from living in bigotry.

However, once we recognize the importance of talking consistently about the effect racism has on people. Hopefully they'll see much clearer how devastating racism affects people's lives, whether you're White or Black? Furthermore, to act shows determination of realizing it blocks out other possibilities of progress, if we lose focus of our objectives to be Unified. However, if we fail to recognize the consequences of having these subjects as part of our way of life. Politicians will continue to suck our blood like a leech from the wounds of neglect, as long as we exist on this Planet.

Obviously, now we seem to be migrating backward from the progress we've made, because of a few individuals want to be recognized as heroes shooting unarmed people in the back. Each day we risk losing the vital importance of our connection as Human-beings. Nevertheless, I believe it's because of their desire to be supreme over who (lives or dies) worldwide!! Sure, I agree those topics may seem boring to talk about among family and friends. Still, we should be obligated to spread our important mission to reevaluate our priorities in our conversations, and find another way other than politics and religion to be United.

Sometimes, I find it hard to ploy conversations people should not ignore. It should be mandatory for all of us to come out of the shadows and join together showing we also believe in ourselves. Letting, our voices be heard, regardless of our differences of faiths and beliefs!! Although, it was written in the Bible, if you make the first step, God will make two steps to help solve the problem!! Unfortunately, we've debated if we're ready to make the first step to change our mental state? To discuss our objectives among family and friends trying to teach the general public what they should know about us. Hoping they're listen or read about what we're really trying to accomplish, which is changing the way we've addressed this death sentencings by guns fire!

Now people are doubtful if we can end this racial problem knowing it would be one of the most challenging efforts to accomplish, since Black people were freed from (slavery). We should also have faith in our ability to accomplish what some politicians are trying to prevent, some Americans from being unified. Further, to be independent of them is having the ability to solve our own problems first, instead of listening to their rhetoric which hasn't changed our abhorrent conditions? First by not making the same mistakes in our decisions politically who we should chose to lead us, aside of their Candidates.

Sure, it will take courage to fight for our independence, being able to celebrate our own Holliday without consent of our oppressors (permission)!! Remember closing our eyes won't be to our advantage to win when we see their violent actions against us are deliberant? Especially, when politicians block the public's demands, and won't create legislation that's suitable to consider. Including, a women's right to choose life or death in her pregnancies to the Embryo she's carrying. Now if they refuse to let women make their own decisions, then we're not as (free) in this Country as we claim to be?

It's time to advocate in our laws, if politicians can't provide change to help Americans, they should stay out of politics, and only you can make that decision by voting! Moreover, we shouldn't forget teaching our children at home and in school, the key word to success is working hard to accomplish it. Just remember, excuses will no longer be tolerated if we don't make this Holiday part of our yearly curriculum on our watch. If we don't apply ourselves correctly, wishful thinking won't gain respect and recognition, now or in the future if we fail!

We must keep fighting until we're recognized in this Country as a force that cannot be stopped, by not understanding it's not politicians' decision, if we fail or succeed, it's (vice-versa)!! It's ironic mostly all we see now on TV and hear on Radio stations are Palm men and women voicing their negative opinions, in everything Black people are trying to accomplish. However, it's sad how inconsiderate it was being there from the lack of courtesy shown to them when they appeared on their show. Interrupting them while they were speaking trying to answer their questions.

What's wrong with our system, when it allows some News Casters to indicate they're the voice of Americans? Or is it just a select group that have an appetite of hearing their obnoxious rhetoric to maintain their so-called high ratings, trying to satisfy their racist viewers? Really, if that kind of attitude continues toward Black men and women, one day it will undoubtedly be challenged through some physical combat. Hopefully that won't be necessary, if future generations of our children, proves the lies said about them and their ancestors aren't based on facts.

Now in our generation reporters are giving praise to Ukrainians who's showing courage in life and death situations. Showing their willing to fight to the death if necessary to gain their freedom from the Russian army. The difference is, it seems some people give no respect to Black people demands, because they want politicians to give them freedom. Without being willing to fight and die for it, like other warriors in different Countries. Unfortunately, no Country will donate weapons to help Black people to win wars, against Countries with nuclear weapons, regardless of their cause for fighting!!

Nevertheless, it's still a sign of weakness sometimes avoiding war against anyone taking their freedom, who's also killing them every-day for (minor crimes)! It makes me Skeptical wondering have politicians also taken a position against everything Americans have fought and died to end discrimination? Now, people are saying it's a question-mark whether if people are paying attention, about the lies talked about Black people. However, I suggest those who really want to know the real story about racism, they should listen to the voices of the dead.

Sure, there may be Americans who's trying to remember the countless deaths Black people spoke about when they were alive. Trying to tell Americans their version of why they're assassinated in the street? I hope Americans won't forget what some politicians said about their Black heroes when they were alive? I remember years ago some politicians said those so-called patriots were acting like traitors and communist when they were alive! (John F. Kennedy Mr. Malcolm X./Dr. Martin L. King Jr and Ms. Harriet Tugman), just to mention a few!!

Yet none of them were accused of being responsible for Millions of Americans dying from misinformation on their quest for freedom. Through the years, trying to reason with politicians is like beating a dead horse saying giddy up, hoping for a miracle to change its condition from a dying Mare to a young Stallion. Obviously, some of these politicians are Meatheads dead from the neck up, from having the kind of leadership and human dignity all Americans can respect.

Moreover, it's worth the effort, just having the satisfaction exposing these republicans documenting the deaths they've caused! How long will Americans be deceived thinking they have absolute control of who governs their destiny? Especially when critics are saying it's the majestic 12 hiding evidence, refusing to teach our children about the massacre of Black Americans over a 100 years ago. It happened in a place called Tulsa the city of Black Wall Street on May 31st 1921. It was tragic how Black people died, without those who were responsible for their deaths, escaped legally from being convicted of genocide.

Through the years, politicians hid their (identity) for Centuries because they were Palms attacking them suddenly in their community without warning. Nevertheless, they suffered and died not knowing their enemy was jealous and envious of them, because they built a community that showed a positive growth financially in their Banks. That's one of many reasons we're living in a system that won't release Black History in their schools' or making it available for our children to read on a consistent basis.

They're constantly failing, to educate people of what happened in the year 1921, concerning the lives of those Black people they wiped out strategically in that era. History will show, their success in business was so unique their competitors at that time couldn't allow Black people to harvest that kind of financial power and live!! Moreover, we shouldn't forget these actions of murder perpetrated by those Palms who violated their right to live, because they were Black geniuses, instead of criminals.

That's why I'm mentioning part of Black history in this book so the next generation of Americans can remember what being Black means to some Americans!! It appears some of the leaders of the Republican party are too cowardly to speak or represent the truth on any level. Yes, after all they've been through together, promise's is the only gratitude politicians offer people of color. Now this Country is allowing White men and women to kill at random any Black person they see without being convicted of the crime!!

Sure, we know, although some politicians pretend, they're not aware some Americans having a problem respecting different Ethnic groups of people! Also, that makes me curious to know the killers of Black people they dumped here from England and other parts of the world in the 15th and 16th century? Can we do a background check to see if they also had criminal records especially of murder!! It's unfortunate although noticeable even now, some Americans hate to use the word separation from their oppressors. Instead of Black Americans realizing they've tried for hundreds of years to keep hope alive concerning that issue.

Still, I don't understand why they feel being with them, will change their condition, when they're (annihilating) them one by one here and overseas?! Finally, my version of what's happening to Black people is available to the public to read and reach their own conclusion, if the validity of what I've written is true or not?! I admit sometimes it hurts when I hear or write about the truth, it surely doesn't always make a difference in people's lives. However, I'm glad racism is exposed to the public, with the understanding how racism has cut deep in the mind and soul of African Americans.

I'm truly grateful, after so many years of waiting, I have the opportunity to write the truth. Now the truth has emerged from the bowers of this Countries existence. Exposing, those involved in this conspiracy to commit crimes, including the KKK who still play a major part in killing and trying to degrade Black people who's trying to change their narrative thoughts to something positive we all can benefit from. Now they realize this problem will never change, if people refuse to accept other human beings as their equal! Sure, it's debatable whether or not Black people are better off now as a Nation in the 21st Century, then their ancestors were Hundreds of years ago?

Now, I've concluded from some of my studies concerning the attitudes of some Black people. It was a repentant feeling trying to understand why some of them are paranoid, especially when they're discussing being separated from their oppressors permanently. Which seems similar to the children of Israel's fear of leaving the Egyptian pharaoh who enslaved them for hundreds of years. I guess some of them don't, feel confident to exist here without Palms being in control of everything they say or do? I wonder have they forgotten, for each inch of progress politicians give them, they take back a (yard of service).

Unfortunately, it seems the majority of Americans are willing to swallow the pill of segregation without speaking against it. Obviously, I think people who fought on the front line in the past and even now on the battlefields of death. Fighting for freedom without weapons, should be considered just as brave as the rest who have guns. Especially if you consider they're still being killed mercilessly on the spot, for reasons that's already mentioned in this book!! The problem is Black Americans are not privileged like Moses to have the (Red Sea Rolled Back) that separates the just from the unjust, trying to es-cape their Pharaoh the (United States)!!

It's unfortunate after all the fighting and dying, racism is still front and center being practiced in those Southern States, prior to them losing the civil war? Still, they're brave enough, to show all Americans why those Southern politicians have dominating and influenced congress to change their voting rules from one section to the next. Knowing they created this negative legislation hoping to deceive the pub-lic!! I know there will be some Americans saying why is he trying to degrade White people, is he also a racist? (The answer is no), if people want to asso-ciate racism with truth tellers believe me, they're barking up the wrong tree.

Suddenly, it came to my attention, this infec-tion of racism is different from all other infections. It's not like having a common cold, with the flu or an operation, that extracts the cancer from one's body so it can function properly. You can believe this or not, once you've been diagnosed with this infection of being a racist it eats away and kills the character of the person you once were. Still these politicians are advocating we're one Nation under

God with liberty and justice for all. Although we know freedom has a price of death attached to it, even from the beginning of America's history!!

Nevertheless, it's hard to accept how some minority groups seem to be reluctant to fight back with the same vigor as they're ancestors. Which reporters refuse to mention in their reporting. The difference is, they fought with their bare hands against guns, and other weapons White men had to defend them-selves against them. Nevertheless, those men showed Bravery fighting fearlessly against the odds, but unfortunately, they died violently because they refused to live in this country as slaves!!

Makes you wonder why aren't there any movies showing those events to Black children using them as mentors they could be proud of? However, reporters are trying to insinuate our ancestors including Mr. Nat, Turner, and his followers was only a fictional story killing seventy of those Palms out of revenge for being treated less than Animals. Still, they hung those Black men for acting defiant against them.

CHAPTER 9

We've been quiet too long.

However, through all the suffering I was asked to be quiet, not to excite more rage about these issues of race. Now I'm elated to say, finally some publishers aren't afraid to publish books giving exposure of what this Country really needs legislatively, Judicially, and Economically. Further, to give equal opportunity, so you would think if Black people aren't killing White supremist who've killed them for centuries. They would refuse to kill anyone who's not a threat to them and their families here?!! That's why Americans, should never forget those republicans who kept our elderly Mothers and Fathers Black and White.

Standing in the streets for hours in freezing Weather throughout the southern part of our Country, trying to prevent them from voting in 2012!! Their effort trying to stop their vote, signals nothing has changed if we elect the republicans in office in 2022. How, would men and women feel, who stood with them in solidarity against freezing weather in 2012. How would you address that problem if our right to vote was erased from the Constitution?!! If you knew Black people you would see so many obstacles that's challenging to overcome. However, until the system makes good paying jobs available, why not deal with this world first, before you think about dying, going to another world?

Unfortunately, there are Christians that can barely provide food for their children on a daily basis. Still they're praying to their god asking for help from being bombarded with other problems forced on them by the system. Now if Americans listen to any republicans' pleas to represent them as president in 2024, it would surely undermine the sacrifices of our fallen veterans who gave their lives believing in our constitution. Yeah, somehow, politicians have the nerve to scold leaders in other countries condemning them of the same crimes they're committing here in America. First, we must understand and acknowledge why politicians are reluctant to change this system that masterfully kept Americans divided for hundreds of years?

We must be on guard from the time we wake up in the morning, until we go to sleep at night, they're always' signifying. It's Black people whose causing all the problems, when we should know that's' not true. The truth is, Black people have always felt optimistic about changing this system period. Furthermore, at times we've heard and seen a lot of negative stories about Native Americans. Palms made movies, about their history revealing how they were hunted down and killed.

I know, it had to be frustrating, for those Black Indians who spoke English listening to palms calling them Savages, while they were trying to protect their land from intruders. Watching them roaming around on their property killing their women and children. Nevertheless, they showed the world, how they used opportunities to annihilate them, and take their land and they were successful. One thing's for sure Indians knew White men speak with fork tongues. They understood and were willing to accept the basics in dealing with their enemies, and their remedy was don't trust them! I understand why those men stood their ground fighting to keep their land out of pride for their-self and their people. Now the results of that war were devastating and degrading for any Human-being, knowing the high price, they're still paying for losing the war.

Well, it shouldn't be hard to believe after all that fighting, their ancestors were forced to live in the desert for centuries. Still without Americans honoring the treaties signed by our government officials to sustain them properly while they are there. Now the rest of us should stop acting naïve about our future with some of these Palms knowing how ruthless they can be when you least expect it?!! Nevertheless, in sight of their problems, some Black people are using religion and Jesus as a crutch to act like cowards, scared to defend their women and children against people who kill them consistently.

It's time they start showing some responsibility in protecting their families in life and death situations, regardless if the killer is in uniform or not!! Through the years I've noticed some police officers won't face Black men violently on equal terms without being armed with a gun!! That's why they continue to be murdered in the streets because Black officers refuse to break the bond with Palms, to act in Black people's defense. The majority of Americans know they are being taken advantage of, still they watch police officers using deadly force against people without enter-fearing. It's obvious some officers think more about their pay check than the value of human life.

Now our children are asking will we continue to hold up meaningless signs without using some physical force in retaliation, to really change the narrative about being killed unarmed? Now, they're tired of listening to people saying some of them are cowards refusing to fight back in self-defense. Now, if you listen, you're hear people asking will violence help stop the killings, a lot of them agreed and some said no to the question? Everyone is saying once they're armed, it would bring relief to so many people who can hardly sleep at night, out of fear of being assassinated by the police. Unfortunately, I've seen more advertisement raising funds for the abuse of Dogs and Cats than for Black families who've experienced the same fate!

However, after all the (oops) killings of Black people, why aren't there any Government relief organizations raising money to help Black families who've lost their children through gun violence? I remember years ago, when the Black Panthers were saying they will defend them-selves against anyone who's using violence threatening their life. Well, immediately thereafter, the system made it very difficult for Black people to own hand guns in the 1950's and 60's and even now.

Politicians were leaving them defenseless saying it was a crime speaking violence because it could cause a riot causing thousands of people to get hurt or killed. Nevertheless, surprisingly they became so efficient in the art of self-defense they outlawed karate for years preventing them to practice the art of self-defense!! Now it's different with White supremacist carrying guns, thanks to Donald J Trump the ex-president. If you're interested to know why this mystery, remains unsolved? It's because these republicans are wearing the word corrupt like a badge of honor to pass down to the next generation.

Sending a message, it's okay to be corrupt as long as they stick together? I read somewhere, one of Donald's family members migrated to America from Germany years ago, should we be concerned about his Ethnic background? I wonder what happens if he does have German DNA, Mr. Trump called President Obama every name in the book concerning his African Heritage. Now I'm convinced these reporters know more about Mr. Trumps background then they're willing to expose to the public. It's ironic when Donald was slurring Mr. Obama's character, the News reporters didn't bother to mention a word about Donald Trump's background.

Not to mention where his wife was born, that makes her different from other immigrants to be called the first lady of this country? Mr. Trump and news reporters did a fact check on everyone except Donald and his wife. It would surely be interesting for all Americans to know his Ethnic background if they really wanted to be fair to Mr. Obama? Moreover, this conundrum he's spreading about his wealth, could be payments for people's silence, about what Mr. Trump is doing that's unethical.

What happened to the American spirit, to produce the kind of information about him their Colleagues would be proud to put in the news? Reporting the truth that's always required in their writings, that will stop people from spreading false information. Instead politicians are engaged in helping people, that's advocating hate thinking that decision will get them reelected to congress. Why can't we have a new voting system called (The people's Choice)? Lately I'm hearing this statement from different generations of young adults saying, they're grown and people should mind their own business. When they refuse to answer requests from their families and friends based on some of the decisions they've made in the past. I hope they're feel the same enthusiasm when they support having a Holiday (African Americans Day)?

Unfortunately, through the years we haven't considered this problem argent enough to solve it!! Actually, we should be tired of asking these politicians to grant Black people a quid-pro-quo policies that could change their grievances on all levels. During my studies about African Americans, there was a statement made, that probably will get a lot of criticism discussing Black history. It was one of those moments I was concerned about discussing this kind of topic. I quote, "How fortunate Black people are being here in (America).

We all know how they suffered being here, it could've been worse if they were living in other countries." However, it turned out I was so frustrated and stunned after hearing that comment I kind of lost control, and blurted out saying, (thankful for what)?! History shows, Black people were dehumanized in every way one could imagine. I said why can't all Americans be grateful just once, for what Black people have accomplished that's helping millions of them in different ways? You may not believe I wished the circumstances were different. So, I write and speak out against negative statements or any actions of violence that should be corrected. First of all, let's be real about this system of politics, when we know some of these southern states are using the words (Battle Ground) States for a reason. I thought the fighting was over, unless we're still fighting a war in the South when the subject matter relates to voting rights!

Look it's important to stay focus, when it's obvious being White in those southern states is the controlling factor whether their votes are counted? Well, the point is, are Americans ready to react to that slogan battleground states as a threat? Or be calm and keep ignoring what that statement means, if we're still at War with them? Let's be clear about what or who they're (battling) just for the record, first it was about slavery, now it's our voting rights. I wonder what's next on their agenda we should be aware of? It's always a struggle looking back, when you see how slave owners received reparation from president Abraham Lincoln after the Slaves were freed.

The records should show, those who owned slaves, received 500 dollars per-single slave/1200 dollars per-family. I guess he felt sympathetic for their loss of property which intitled them to be compensated after being insured because Black people were considered as (cargo). Imagine traveling in those packed conditions on ships? Now I realize how important it is having control of the ballad boxes that still gives those minority states the advantage to decide who wins elections. However, people are saying we've acted too passive giving such power to those minority southern states to dictate who and when Americans can or can't vote?

Now it seems the power of the people have lost that strong grip they once had on the decision making in this country. Now, for years we've accepted these politicians' failures to do their jobs without being incarcerated for misleading the public.

Especially when they lie about what they've done to help the general public to succeed. Now when I think about how hard my Ancestors prayed trying to visualize the future with hope of equal opportunity for them and all Americans. I admit it makes me angry their efforts were considered by politicians, as insignificant, and a waste of their time. Even now the mental stress of their oppressors has survived against some Americans, and politicians seem to be elated.

While their dancing victory laps against our Ancestors and all Americans in this modern world of lies and deceit!! Now Americans are saying the system is rigged, in determining who or where they can go to hear the truth? Yes, I know this is another complaint in the suggestion box that will probably be ignored just like the rest of our complaints. Now, the feeling is, if 400 years wasn't enough time to resolve a problem of this magnitude, it will never be solved. Think about it, because it's a fair statement to consider, especially, when there's been very little improvement in that area.

Maybe they're right and all of us should grow up and face facts, and don't forget what we've seen every-day, nothing but corruption and lies to confuse the public. If we're not ready to solve this problem now, Americans should look in the mirror and be honest? We should be acknowledging justice can't take action, when it's blinded by corruption and can't (see) those individuals perpetrating the crime! Especially, after waiting all these years, hoping this imaginary dream would come true, trying to have equality in this Country is like trying to hit the lottery? Now who's to blame for the delay, of all this talk about justice for all, I think it should be reevaluated as a (scam)? Why can't we admit, it's not logical believing anything politicians say after 400 hundred years of waiting?

Nevertheless, I know it's impossible for this kind of breed, to show remorse for their deadly actions of violence, that's why politicians continue to use voter blockers to make it difficult for dark skinned people to vote?! Furthermore, writing my side about this dilemma helps to balance my decision for writing this book!! Unfortunately, if we don't know by now justice shouldn't only exist on a piece of paper that can be cast aside, depending on the mood politicians are in, from one day to the next? Still, it should matter to Americans who are real patriots, who's not willing to serve this god, the U.S. Especially, without having some morals and principles attached to it, concerning who should lead us in the future)?!!

CHAPTER 10

Can Prayer really Change Things?

Let me be clear, I guess it's okay to serve any god you choose as long as it doesn't hurt or kill someone because of envy or jealousy. I've heard most politicians claim to have some religious background, now if that's true we shouldn't have these kinds of problems with politics, religion, and racism, without seeing some positive results. Through my studies, pioneers of this country were willing to give their lives to guide, protect and maintain positive ideas as a pathway to their family's success, and for others to follow!! It's unfortunate the only lives that seem to matters are the ancestors of those Confederate soldiers that fought and died under their Flag of Slavery.

Now we've seen the rage of these people at the capital and it wasn't a pretty sight, when you see them holding a Confederate Flag yelling Donald's Trumps name as their leader. These are the same disputes we thought were settled hundreds of years ago that caused a civil war!! We know these civilian traitors were rebelling like this for decades, hiding in the woods pledging their allegiants to the confederate flag!! Nevertheless, for years we've seen these animals only prey on defenseless people of different backgrounds who's unarmed.

Which leaves their children also vulnerable to die, from the playgrounds they play in, and the schools they attend. Or while they're asking questions about why it's taking so long for adult Christians to end this racial problem?!! I guess they'd rather remain silent about this or show more interest being in church on time instead of participating with other patriots. Trying to think of ideas to fight and win without killing people, by using other platforms of advertisement to spread what truthtellers are trying to accomplish! It's time for all Americans to show a sense of responsibility to the next generation before things get worse. If not, I don't see a positive future for anybody, whether you're a liberal or a conservative!

I've heard critics are skeptical trying to establish who to believe, the so called righteous that believe in Jesus, or the so called unrighteous they're trying to convince are going to Hell, if they refuse to follow their religious doctrine? Which leaves people reaching the conclusion there is no verbal connection between (God and Man)! That's why we've been killing each other for centuries failing, thinking we're communicating with Him? Let's face it, these so-called Christians who don't have a rational explanation of why their prayers about racism and the killings of Black people weren't answered in 400 plus years?

After all this time they should understand, if Gods actions speaks louder than words, of doing absolutely nothing to help solve this problem? My response is maybe we should pay attention, and do what's necessary to stop it our-selves? Sure, I understand and accept breaking news has always caused discomfort for some people hearing or reading about these controversial subjects for the first time. The question is, are we ready for what's ahead in this modern age of young minds, who won't feel intimidated hearing or reading about the truth regardless of who or where it came from!!

I understand after writing and speaking about this unholy revelation, there's a price to pay. Especially, when you're willing to sacrifice your life and the love of your family and friends to tell the truth. Further, carrying this heavy cross trying to endure the brunt of separation from those who's supposed to love you unconditionally? Nevertheless, it's not easy trying to connect with people believing there's a mystical world somewhere unseen. That theory is what keeps us devastated, wondering if there's a world that exist physically and spiritually, compelling us to die to get there?

Unfortunately, no one knows the answer how this new revelation affects people, that refuse to adhere to the truth. It's time to stop believing sooth-sayers, who advocate these lies just to get their tied money, telling people God demands ten percent of their income? However, it's really disturbing know-ing some of us are willing to ignore facts in deter-mining what is truth in their debates concerning these issues of faith and beliefs?! Yeah, their religious beliefs have caused more confusion and anger and it's driving some so-called Christians to stay away from their family members, and friends.

Well, it's because their faith wasn't designed to share their income with those who have the same DNA! Nevertheless, I guess it's okay for them to feel that way, obviously it's because they're afraid of knowing their Jewish God, is causing the deaths of Millions of people here and in different parts of the world. Still, some Americans have to be reminded that facts matter, whether you're a Jew, or Gentile? I know some of them have been misled so long by Ministers and politicians, it's hard to disbelieve someone you've trusted all your life to tell the truth about life after death! Now when you look at their records it indicates, there's been a pattern of excuses and false promises made by politicians and others to keep us separated, which is part of the concept (divide and conquer).

Further, all of us should know by our experiences, to put your trust in no man, for they all will deceive you, according to what's written in the Bible! So, when we talk about dying, let's stop lying about where we're going after death if we're not following the rules that will guide you there. We know this isn't a new story, talking about Jesus is coming back for us when some of us can't restrain their-selves from killing each other. Just speaking for myself, I know the percentages of this system being fair to people is only a myth. Nevertheless, that's why Palms created laws when they're accused of lying, by taking the fifth when they're guilty of committing an unlawful act.

That's the method politicians used in court, nipping those charges at the bud without lying further. That's why, as an Author myself I try to expose lies when others won't, especially when people's lives are at-stake!! Through the years I've seen the financial support these politicians receive from Millionaires and Billionaires, which is the link that continues to overpower the majorities point of view to eliminate all chances of them being able to succeed. They're, always, using their money to control the economic growth which gives them a huge advantage against their opponents who's just trying to survive with minimum wages!! So, with your support we have a chance to save lives through Authors who's willing to write telling the world about the other side of life that so many Americans haven't experienced. Especially, living through the kind devastation others have barely survived during their lifetime.

I know some people will say I've read about these same issues for years, what's his point? Unfortunately, my point is all of this confusion started from those 3 subjects, politics, religion and racism!! I guess it's because it's rarely mentioned in the news about their lack of exposing those 3 subjects that's proven to be detrimental to our youth in America. I concur what was said by knowledgeable people, about (experience) being the best teacher. If that's true their records should indicate Black people have 400 plus years of experience dealing with racism and corrupt politicians!!

That's why I'm still waiting for Americans Black and White, to support in solidarity a Holiday mentioned earlier in this book!! Although, it may not be easy to gain all of their support for it to be successful, especially if they refuse to cooperate knowing it's well deserved. Moreover, it would be a sad day not just because I'm asking for their support, it would also reflect Americans lack of gratitude for their services rendered. Naturally, to honor and remember what this Holiday would mean to Millions of Americans who've sacrificed, the honor of having their ancestors last (name)! In my opinion all Americans should see this well-lit reflection of how some Americans died including president Abraham Lincoln.

Also let's not forget those brave Union Soldiers Black and White who fought and won for all Americans to enjoy that unquenchable thirst for freedom. Meanwhile, we're still trying to recover from another catastrophe ex-president Obama had to fix years ago. However, it's hard for me to accept, why News' reporters haven't mentioned it on their TV shows in years? Still some people haven't forgotten the one who started this huge economic catastrophe. I guess being a Republican has its privileges, for disregarding facts, or not choosing to remember these life changing events, by shieling the mistakes he made both militarily and economically. Coupled with other misstates reporters won't mention, which is not keeping Americans safe during the 911 invasion.

It was ex-president (Gorge W. Bush) who failed to protect and perform his duties as president. Nevertheless, he's still receiving support from those News Media stations and from politicians who gave Mr. Bush a pass. Further, by not holding him accountable for the mess he created, and left to ex-President Obama to solve trying to capture Osama bin Ladin. I guess republicans were so busy criticizing Mr. Obama in everything he said in public, telling people they hoped he failed, still that didn't stop him from accomplishing his goals. However, if we weren't paying attention, we wouldn't have seen politicians' refusal to stop their Colleagues from trying to humiliate him in public!

I know they won't admit it now because some of them are cowards with a vengeance. Knowing ex-president Obama accomplished positive legislation that helped Millions of Americans to survive with his solution, (Obama Care)! Hopefully, I guess out of conscience I'm quite sure after Mr. Obama has passed on physically. Great conversations about him will emerge from the muddy water's politicians created trying to drown and dishonor him for being one of the greatest presidents in American History!! So, my point is, it doesn't matter what position or accomplishments Black people contribute to this country.

It's obvious, there will always be a political loophole that gives Palms an opportunity through T.V, Radio, and internet to try and degrade them. It seems being envious isn't enough for those who's jealous, seeing a Black person accomplish so much without them contributing to their success!! For years we've ignored speaking about that trail of death Black people suffered, now politicians are reluctant to talk about how degrading it was being a slave. It's obvious, some of them are willing to accept the benefits of the past that involved slavery and racism, instead of trying to make a difference legislatively to make sure that kind of suffering doesn't happen in the future.

Hey, you can be sure it's still occurring in cities and states across this country, while the majority of politicians remain silent showing defiance in their speeches, ignoring the tragedies that's occurring every day. I understand why immigrants feel so comfortable and thankful for being here in the U.S. I believe it's because they weren't restricted from speaking their own languages, without incident from the Government, that granted their visa. I know it would be challenging for them to admit, if they were the victims being treated less than Human-beings? Erasing their Ethnic identities and Culture further causing their deaths by hangings just because they existed differently from those who ruled in this Country.

Which further prevented them and others alike from exercising their right if just for a moment to know and participate in the same lifestyle of their Ancestors!! For years, we've ignored White men were the Frankenstein's of African Americans. Further by creating a new life being here/a new identity, and death to serve a new Country, if they didn't obey. Now these Palms are afraid wanting to kill some of these so-called Black monsters jogging around in their communities in different states! I must admit the word (Nigga) is just another word for some people to describe a Monster instead of a Human-being. Obviously, it doesn't matter, if some Americans are not willing to admit what they really feel about them.

They also, have the nerve trying to hide the facts from our youth, Black and White, of the sac-rifices and the disrespect shown to them, since they were brought here from Africa. They also had the task trying to make difficult decisions to stay alive without acting violent in a physical way. Which would've had a deadly result for them because they were unarmed to defend them-selves. Further Black men had to consider and control their emotions fac-ing terror seeing their women being raped in front of them, at a time when White supremacist ruled over them!!

Now at my age writing about this issue isn't easy to control my emotions of how far we've come as a people without a country that's willing to treat all Americans with the same respect. My question is how would Palm immigrants know about Black peoples struggles. Unless they read about them in books written by historians who didn't always reveal the hold truth about the kind of conditions they survived in? Now they have a lot of negative things to say about Black people without sharing the griefs and pain of helping to give birth to a new Country that turned against them violently. Now I'm wondering, where were their families when there was no justice for Black people after giving their lives fighting for freedom in the civil war?!!

What part did these White immigrants contribute in freeing and defeating those who were slave owners? Well, it's been a while since we've seen reporters talk about, when Black people fought and died in their Countries, because they also were a threat to our way of life as Americans! Tell me are they going to offer their services to protect me, when men and women right now fear for my safety because of the important narratives being repeated and exposed in this book? It's really unfortunate and frustrating for them wondering why the hope line to receive justice for them seems to be longer today, then yesterday?

However, in the midst of all of this negativity, I've heard people saying if they had to go through what Black people have endured, they wouldn't want to be an American!! That said let's turn this chapter of inequality and try to think pessimistically. Especially, about the ideas of the majority of Americans trying to reform the system. From an over whelming number of politicians who do nothing to help Americans succeed except for the rich. So, brace yourself, there will be more battles ahead with politicians fighting against giving the public a (15-dollar) minimum wage. Just like their leader Donald Trump they have the audacity to prevent people from earning extra money to provide for their families.

We all know fifteen dollars and hour isn't much of a raise after 60 years, of earning one dollar hour in the nineth-tenth century! Knowing politicians have earned a lot more since then?! Furthermore, it shouldn't matter if these politicians we elect are White or Black. What matters, if they're qualified to be leaders by giving every American an equal (opportunity) to succeed? We know this wouldn't be tolerated if Black leaders kept Americans in these trapped conditions for Hundreds of years. Especially, with the KKK and other supremacist groups rebelling showing aggression to kill people if they didn't change the system.

Let's be (real) about our ex-president Mr. Barack Obama who performed magnificently in a crisis. Now you would think these politicians and all Americans would owe Mr. Obama a great deal of gratitude. For bringing our economy back to normal, while dealing with so much stress from politicians who wanted him to fail? Now they'd rather spend hours talking about the failed efforts of Mr. Trump trying to overthrow our government. Unfortunately, he's still instigating talking about how corrupt Democrats are, without having any credible evidence to support his claims. It's ironic how rarely they mention Mr. Obama's name in contrast to Mr. Trump, the man with no conscience!!

However, for years I've seen people claiming to be Christians in church voting for corrupt politicians!! Still, It's not ethical teaching their children to follow a man named Jesus, and they follow other men who's totally different in character according to the Bible? It's a shame after the singing/preaching and shouting is over in church, they become a totally different person on their way home. Showing their children who they really are as human-beings, advocating and following one of Satan's most devout advocators of lies and deceit. Although we're not that, naïve to think corruption started with Donald Trump.

Sure, we've fought corruption in our political, and judicial system for centuries. Knowing some Judges, and politicians of both parties', are saying they're rendering justice, while being affiliated with that mob the KKK if not in body but in thought. Unfortunately, instead of politicians stopping that mob after the Union Army defeated those southern rebels, they were being complicit pretending they were (innocent) of the complaints they were accused of. Since the war, the only time these killers showed fear, is when president Obama threated to take some of their guns away. It seems, their symbol of White supremacy is obviously accepted in these battleground states by the police and their political leaders.

We should know wishful thinking hoping to solve these problems of violence is not the solution. Especially, when they said in the 18th century the war was over after the Confederate soldier General Lee surrendered to General Grant. It's really disturbing, that whatever agreement they signed between the North and South didn't change Black people's condition, then and even now in some parts of the

South!! Just look around, instead of them wearing white sheets over their heads they're wearing police uniforms killing people. I must say, it's not difficult to understand why this country is so wicked after seeing so many faith goers in church every Sunday?

Obviously, some of them use their god as a camouflage hiding their true character of being none other than cold-blooded killers? Or is it possible prayer have its priorities knowing who's changeable from those who's not? The only purpose for me writing this book is to tell the truth to anyone who's interested in knowing about these ongoing tragedies that could've been avoided. If only we had the guts to speak out knowing it wouldn't take 400 years to fix anything if Americans really wanted to end this problem!!

CHAPTER 11

Does the Truth Matter or not?

Now's the time these news casters show enough backbone to ask these southerners. Why they believe they're more patriotic than the Ancestors of those who won the war against the confederate army?! In contrast to what happened at the Capital news reporters should stop talking about how angry and terrible those protesters were for burning buildings. I guess they were tired of seeing unarmed men being shot in the back in broad day-light running away from gun fire. It's ironic how their comments changed, when police officers were being threatened and attacked at the Capital.

They were acting afraid with their weapons to protect Americans against hundreds of armed White men. Sometimes I wonder, when Black people protest burning buildings, why they summoned the National guard with tanks to control the heated temperament between them and the police. Believe me, it's all a (sham)!! We must understand before we allow these violent acts to continue, *this is a pivotal moment in our history*, to decide who we are defensively to stop their aggression? Especially if we're confused trying to decide whose leadership we're willing to accept, as an example for our children to follow.

While, trying to show them a Blueprint of conduct to guide and protect them in a crisis? Further, being put in situations not expecting palms to use profanity and the word Nigger, as another description of who they are personally. Some Palms have no idea how devastating even now to hear someone using language that insensitive around children changing their hold perspective about people. So, if these Palms were confined receiving therapy, maybe that would eliminate a lot of problems. I'm sure it's better our children are aware of the problems Black people face every day. Giving them a chance to make their own decisions if what they read about these people is credible to believe or not.

However, after experiencing all of this madness we know these teachings about those three subjects won't stop them from brainwashing our children in the future, if it's not exposed to the public! There's an old saying, a (wise man) changes but a fool never changes. I'm not trying to pacify anyone's feeling to divert them from the truth, knowing this issue was ignored too long, to complain about reading or hearing people talking about these problems now. To discuss or vote on a new method other than politics and religion to unify us. Nevertheless, we're at a time when you speak or write about the truth it seems to have an antagonistic effect on people.

Once again let me be clear I don't claim to be a Holy or a righteous person. I'm just trying to help people decide what path to follow, either facts or fiction. So, I'm asking everybody, take a minute of your time and think about the kind of people we were in the past, and who we are striving to be as Americans?!! Unfortunately, I'm ashamed to admit a lot of Americans haven't accepted the true value of our constitutional laws that should bind us together. Instead, we've allowed these southerners to be acknowledged as patriots, although we know they're nothing but fear Mongers trying to scare the public!

History will show Palms always had a problem following the rules, trying to prevent Americans from knowing who they are really aside of being politicians. You know, for me its mind boggling, when you talk about privileged being a White man or woman in this country, is an understatement to say the least!! Now I've concluded, if the majority of

Americans prefer to see bravery when it's used with a gun against unarmed people. Then you don't know what it means to be brave and to have the courage to fight unarmed?!! It doesn't seem to matter how the rest of Americans are treated trying to confront their problems differently from White people!

I want to alert Christians of all denominations if they knew what these politicians were doing to Black people and didn't say or do anything to stop it? Questions would be appropriate to ask what kind of God are they serving? However, it would appear they're making it compelling for others to believe in (Atheism) if He allows this kind of injustice against Black people to continue? Especially when there's no evidence, they were brutalized being attacked by Black people while the police were supposedly performing their duties! Americans, believed after the Gorge Floyd trial police officers' acts of violence and murder would no longer be tolerated in this Country.

Moreover, if you think about it, the evidence is clear police officers kill some people for the sport of it, that's what the public should know for their own safety! Moreover, Americans should be grateful, president Joe Biden finally signed in Law, Juneteenth a National Holiday, ending slavery in this country centuries ago. However, will that document heal the wombs, changing the heart/mind and soul of White men and women in those deep southern states? Having that Holiday Juneteenth is a reminder of the past, but it doesn't speak collectively for all Americans heroes that were seen and unseen.

Who contributed everything, being forced to relinquish their African identity to stay alive. Furthermore, we know their acts of heroism wasn't documented in their history books, because some politicians didn't want to face public scrutiny about their negative actions past and present. Furthermore, giving this Holliday, that's already mentioned in this book will include everybody collectively known and unknown to be honored for their (sacrifice). So, I'm suggesting, if Black people really want something that's denied, then organize and take a stand and refuse to participate in any activities on that date once a year. Even losing one day's work would be worth the sacrifice to show unity among Black and White Americans. This Holliday is about showing (respect) for all Americans past and present who deserves that honor!

These politicians know it's true, but some of them don't give a damn one way or the other if we (succeed) or fail to make improvements! Hopefully, those who read this book will also honor them by spreading the word in case the public haven't heard about this Holiday from the main stream media!! Remember, the constitution didn't specify a specific group of Americans the right to vote or to bear arms!! I'm sure our (enemies) here and overseas would love to see us divided over that dispute. It seems republicans are doing a better job trying to change everything our Ancestors fought and died for.

Those who've paid attention know, the only chance we have to succeed, is by giving Americans of all colors equal opportunities to work in different fields of employment. Yes, politicians know it won't happen if Americans refuse to vote for politicians who's willing to abide by our Constitutional Laws without prejudice. Also, it would change some of our abhorrent immoral conduct, that's being perpetrated by politicians whose strategy is to keep some Americans drowning in these high waves of poverty.

It's always a constant battle, trying to reason with politicians who's determine to block Blacks and other groups of Americans from being accepted socially. Especially Black Athlete who's participating in sports, being denied the curtesy of not listening to disrespectful racial slurs. Especially from individuals in the audiences that continues to echo their views about them far and wide in their professional careers. Yeah, if Americans would just consider the possibilities of a different world without the same barriers allowing intruders in their communities to attack them while they sleep.

So, buckle up, these laws must be changed by politicians making it almost impossible for us to live together socially without conflict!! There's one thing I'm looking forward to as an old man that gives me hope for the future, it's my faith in Humanity. Yes, it's time to admit and understand, this small portion of good and righteous behavior some of these politicians are practicing, isn't as innocent in their social gatherings as you may think?

However, it wouldn't be logical, for any prudent thinking person to believe based on their prior history, politicians' minds aren't polluted. Mixed with false Ideologies that's, convincing some Americans they've been converted from being corrupt over night? What's so troubling is they're Constantly showing malice and deceit, and we're hoping to see a different version of who they are really, other than Palm men and women we can't trust. However, if we're that gullible to believe they've changed from their racial mentality when they refuse to acknowledge or abide by what their ancestors wrote in the Constitution.

Then I suggest you should do more research concerning the actions of politicians you've voted for in the past?!! This egregious lack of duty by them has become somber and unpatriotic knowing the outcome could result in more tragedies. So, why are we willing to declare war on other Nations that threatens our Democracy, but won't declare war on Americans who refuse to abide by our Constitutional laws?! It's obvious nothing has changed from these years of waiting for these politicians to grant what some Americans need to survive.

Also, it's time to act, knowing even when people aren't fighting the system politically, they're fighting it judiciously every day in their prisons. For those who don't know, Black men and women are always fighting from being the majority in their prisons. Letting our courts invoke more punishment working them receiving slave wages of 50-cents or less a day, in different categories in prison. The question is, why they haven't reported that to the public, so they can increase their wages so when they release them from prison, (they're have a better chance to succeed)?!!

It's no secret, the only problem that's holding Black people from achieving their goals, in America and around the world, are White men and women who's constantly trying to degrade them!! It seems just their presence poses a threat to Palms, either from Envy/Jealousy or both? If you believe otherwise, you've ignored the foul things they've endured for the past 400 years. For hundreds of years Palm men have killed Black men and young boys who've flirted with White women in the South, and in different parts of this nation)?!

It should be obvious when they put people through so much pain and agony, without showing any remorse being consistent with aggression to harm them, they should be in prison. Just think back years ago, you're see the same aggression hasn't changed, when they see darker skinned men flirt with White women. However, if you really believe they're killing Black people because they really fear for their lives, or just using those words as some sinister excuse to commit Murder?! Everyone who've seen these acts of murder should speak out, knowing they're not wearing a mask or sheets over their heads hiding their faces, if they're engaging in something noble to help people who's suffering.

Unfortunately for them, Uncle Sam, is still pointing his finger asking Black men and women to join their military. Knowing they will go overseas and be harassed and disrespected by a majority of Palm men and women in uniform, giving some of them suicide Missions. Obviously, after Black Soldiers complete their mission reporters say nothing about their heroic acts on the battlefield!! Now we realize this isn't the time to be silent about this, when politicians know the ones Black people should be warring against are right here killing them.

Unfortunately, no one is asking questions, or concerned about politicians monitoring their families on their job's while their Black siblings are fighting and dying overseas? More than likely, these are the people politicians' prey on financially for help. Furthermore, we know politicians have a reputation of being generous with their Tax money to help other Countries in wars. That's why they refuse to increase minimal wages for our workers here, and that's really something to consider when politicians ask for your vote. I was asked, why I keep blaming White politicians in congress for the problems some Americans are having?

It's, because they control the House and the Senate as the majority vote, of what legislations are passed in Congress! If we keep floundering around acting naïve, more stressful conditions will occur. Unfortunately, we're still allowing only White civilians to be judge/jury and executioners of Black people, because they thought without sufficient evidence a crime was committed? Just think about the promises made to Americans for centuries without politicians showing any effort to solve their grievances.

Unfortunately, they know having (weapons), would give them more respect than fighting unarmed protesting trying to reason with people who seem to be unethical? Why aren't the police and politicians threatening White protesters with Tanks to be (nonviolent?) I guess they're reluctant to admit, if they were willing to participate in an insurrection at the Capital believing a lie about the election. Who knows what would've happened if those battleground states had setup barricades within the political system preventing them from voting?!!

I hate to predict all the prayers we offer to God won't change some of these peoples' negative behavior. I believe 400 years of waiting for it to stop proves their efforts to change, hasn't been affective enough to save lives. Just to remind Christians, I hope they know their prayers failed to make a difference in the lives of Black people, yet they continue believing things will work it-self out, without realizing it doesn't take God 400 years to change their condition? I realize hope comes with the possibility of change, but it's obvious that's not possible dealing with that kind of breed, always having the instinct to kill instead of showing empathy for people who disagrees with their policies?!!

CHAPTER 12

Is this a racist country?

I admit fame or fortune has its place, what I'm more concerned about is leaving this problem of racism to my children and grandchildren to solve. Sometimes I worry, when I no longer have a voice to speak or the use of my hands to write about how important this problem is, to fight against. I hope they will grab the Baton of equality fighting hard to win the race against those politicians who've prevented our progress for centuries. Its ironic politicians are willing to spend billions of taxpayers' money to land on the moon in an Atmosphere they can't survive without Oxygen. Why would that mission take priority over solving people being killed here every-day? In light of what they're doing, that money could be used, to help dissect racism from the hearts and minds of their oppressors?

Politicians spend our Tax money, without an explanation to justify the slow process they're using to land on Mars. Does anyone know, how Americans benefit financially from Astronauts walking on Mars, which hasn't of sixty or more years been achieved? Ask your-self have politicians showed Americans any prof, we're all in this (together)? When they disregard people who can't put food on their tables or stop the courts from ruining their children's lives with paper felonies that's hard to fight against legally? Especially when politicians feel walking on the moon is more important, than saving the lives of our youth from violence and death?!

Its heartless when politicians don't feel those problems are argent enough to solve first, before they venture into space. Although we know it's not easy to pass anything if the majority of politicians are acting partisan concerning that issue. Nevertheless, after all this time you would think people wouldn't be waiting patiently, without politicians showing any signs they can end these problems we've fought against for centuries. Unfortunately, they're always listening to their leaders, telling them to keep hoping when there's no sign of change!

I don't understand why they're waiting to Exit those Southern states permanently? Moreover, when they know it's a matter of life and death to protect their families! Yes, those are battleground states, and the only ones dying by the thousands in that part of this country are (Black people). Sure, some of them have a history in those states of unspeakable sadness, that makes them feel a sense of heritage being there. Although I understand why Blacks stay there fighting, out of respect to honor their ancestors. Who struggled with the same problems or worse hundreds of years ago.

This isn't a new story I feel proud writing about when the price of death is always' hanging in the balance. Death seems to be waiting for those whose brave enough to speak against politicians who's corrupt, causing more grief in the world. Yes, if most White families felt the same pressure of being killed by police officers because of the color of their skin, I know this problem would've taken 400 years to solve. For years we haven't discussed the effect it has on our youth being scared to leave home. Which causes them to Fail trying to concentrate on their school assignments. Nevertheless, they're graded by their teachers without considering the distractions, and the pressure they're facing every day trying to stay alive.

In which has caused some of them to act violent being accused of committing crimes knowing their families can't afford to pay lawyers to represent them properly in court! It's unfortunate, the door that hid the skeletons of corruption, weren't opened this wide until Mr. Donald J Trump became president. Critics, are saying they are overwhelmed, that if there's any Justice, those responsible for millions of Americans dying from the Corona-virus should be avenged. However, if that crime didn't open the eyes of Justice, then nothing we write or say will change our direction from the way it has been. Now these politicians are becoming bolder by the minute putting their second amendment rights to the forefront, refusing to prosecute those perpetrators that left millions of people in mourning!!

Obviously, what those politicians have done in my view should be recognized beyond criminality, it should be categorized and delt with as trying to commit premeditated Murder against humanity? However, we're still waiting for the results of their investigation of Donald Trump and his party who helped perpetrate this evil crime. Please don't forget, the more republicans act innocent of crimes there's one thing we know, they were lying while they were in office. Just like they're doing now about the election and the treatment needed to cure the Corona-virus. Hey, it's unbelievable how Mr. McConnell isn't held accountable for his involvement with Mr. Trump's scam, still he remains in office. Yes, it's no secret he's just as guilty as Mr. Trump for helping him as a conspirator to the crime.

However, we know where his support is coming from, it's mainly from the deep South? It's not his fault he's in office, all of us should share the blame for allowing him to be voted in Congress. Now he's showing his gratitude saying, they're mission is not to help but to obstruct what President Joe Biden is doing to end this crisis. The question is, who Americans prefer to lead them, a Dictator they can't trust in contrast to a Democracy? Now the wheel of time is spinning wondering why they allowed some of these so-called patriots to adapt Hitler's philosophy of White supremacy in this country? Or was this philosophy being practiced here for centuries, that only Black Americans could recognize beneath this deceitful cloud of deception advocating justice for all?

Don't forget, we might've defeated the Germans in a physical war years ago, when Hitler ruled that part of the world, saying the Germans were the superior Race. Unfortunately for him, History will reflect they totally failed to prove that in sports and in battle. So, after waiting all these years there shouldn't be any excuses that could justify why we haven't ended that negative concept of supremacy forever in our society? Some of our leaders are acting so corrupt anything is possible having a (nuclear war) if we fail to unite? Knowing the problems, we're having now wouldn't matter if we survived that catastrophe?

However, if we don't act with authority to change those antiquated southern philosophies of White supremacy. It would trigger off an annihilation of the Human race! I repeat, all of us should teach our children at home about what their struggle has been for centuries, before they go to their schools. I know fighting against this mental condition is more important to think about, and I hope some White people won't go there, forcing people to kill or be killed in order to survive.

It's not easy to maintain, nonviolent acts when you're constantly being threaten trying to satisfy politicians who's not subjected to the same conditions. It's hard when Black people have the task to figure out, what's their alternatives while they're running away from gun fire. Especially when they're trying to stay alive, when police officers Black and White are joined together using force trying to kill them?!! We should know by now when these racist police officers kill them, they make sure there's no witnesses. Including their families are unable to testify in their defense in court pertaining to what happened at the scene of the crime.

Obviously, nothing has changed, because some Black police officers won't witness to facts the way it really happened. They're strategy is to blocked the public from seeing police officers report or videos immediately after it happened on the scene? (Why), because we know the police are always protected legally by their Unions and the Courts, even if they're guilty of committing murder. They slow down their investigation process to aid and a-bet hiding evidence, giving the police absolute advantage over families of dead Black men and women whose grieving.

I would relish the idea of one day Americans will stop warring period especially against each other. Fighting and dying because of their different views about both subjects' politics/racisms. Hopefully history won't show, we were defeated by a minority group of southerners advocating racism and discrimination. It seems we've lost that instinct of determining who's the enemy and the patriots are really in this country? I've also noticed when Americans are praying to God waiting for His help, and when He doesn't respond to their request.

Most Americans refer their problems to (politicians) to solve for them, instead of using a prudent strategy to solve their own problems. Why can't we admit some of them still rely on incompetent politicians because they're of the same (Origin)! Sadly, with all due respect I must express what I've felt over

60 years about some of these fake so-called White patriots who's always causing chaos. Honestly, these politicians are so afraid of losing an Empire they don't own. Still, they're willing to crush the owners, which is the American people to gain power.

Now it's time to withdraw this long leash we've allowed these racist individuals to use and defecate over everything Black and White American patriots have contributed to this country!! Look at this, if Black Americans want to forgive their oppressors, still feeling those words in a song applies to them? Singing my Country tis of the, sweet land of (liberty), I guess it's okay. However, one verse in that song truly relates to Black people which is the land where our (fathers died). Why? Because most of their lives were spent fighting against oppression in a system that allowed Palms to own Black people as property for hundreds of years.

Just look around and listen to what some of your White neighbors are talking about? Maybe you should ask, will they be willing to sacrifice their heritage of owning slaves that gained their wealth through slavery? I have no doubt you're be disappointed with their response! It's obvious this conspiracy to keep Black people totally depended on their oppressors began when they were stripped of their identity. Knowing they were committing a Felony according to their laws of (Kidnaping). Holding them Hostage against their will, not allowing them to retreat back to their home land in Africa.

I believe their strategy was keeping them here long enough to erase their memories of what part of Africa they came from, and what tribe they belonged to. It was an ingenious plan that worked by giving them foreign names and threatening death, if they spoke their Native tongue. Which helped to eliminate all traces between Black slaves and their home in Africa. Unfortunately for them none of their tribesmen searched for them to bring them back to Africa.

Nevertheless, it made it easier for White men to maintain control over them especially with all the powerful weapons they had to use against them if they rebelled. How can anyone in their right mind say this isn't a racist country when the evidence of hangings and shootings of Black people proves it? We should think about if they're using that as a trick question to test and expose Black men and women who still have the guts to tell the truth. I suggest those who don't fear them should be careful, they may be coming for you (next)?!

CHAPTER 13

Don't believe everything you hear

Yes, I can also sympathize with other immigrants who lived here all their lives contributing positively to this country, also risking their lives in wars fighting against other Nations. Yeah, all of us have a story to tell, about these politicians here and in different countries with their diabolical false promises of hope some Americans never received. Nevertheless, now people want to see change in their representation from Americans who won't discriminate against them. Yeah, if that building in Washington D.C is really the peoples house instead of the White house, then call it the people's house?

Let's, be clear because it's very confusing trying to understand if it's the peoples house, or just a building painted (White)? However, all these years I've wondered if there's a sinister hidden message in the color of that building, they show so much pride for Palms saying it. Obviously, it's the color that really matters to some people, who refuse to call it the people's house?!! Politicians makes it difficult to hear the voices of our ancestors telling us to change the way we think about politics and their religious beliefs, when some of them don't adhere to their god's messages? Sure, some Americans refuse to admit the Creator allows people to survive under these conditions to speak truth, through those He's chosen to be messengers, whether we approve of them or not.

Yes, I agree, they should know from prior experiences of learning the hard way, listening to politicians who refuse to stand in their shoes momentarily out of respect to understand what they're going through. How much longer will we wait, holding up signs saying BLM, knowing just saying those words isn't enough to be effective without some physical action to protect our own. I must admit from my perspective, violence seems to be the only method used for them to be at peace with other Nations. Nevertheless, having that savage instinct to kill seems to be part of some Americans DNA, if it's not animals or birds they're hunting with guns, its Human-beings.

It makes me wonder who's next on their agenda of (undesirables)? Or could it be some of our visitors from outer space they can't wait to kill, after they learn more about their advancement in weaponry and technology? However, if that's what's influencing Americans to believe politicians are trustworthy, with the lives of others who's different? Then, you don't have a clear understanding of how this country was built!! The question is, where are the safety zones for Black Americans who just want to go about their lives in peace?! Unfortunately, if Americans keep warring against each other, they will lose their way intellectually of having unity on this planet?!

I guess to some Americans this gift of life God gave them seems to be taken for granted. Letting Millions of Americans die unnecessarily from the Corona-virus, and those who's killing unarmed people in the streets. Unfortunately, we don't know if God will punish these evil doers while we live, or wait for judgment day to pass judgement according to the Bible? I wonder if this new punishment will be as effective after death, as it appeared to be while we're physically alive? Now when we use death as the ultimate penalty for committing a crime, it seemed to be effective, because we all feared crossing that line, if we wanted to live?!

Yes, I was advised by my Elders not to question God's decisions concerning who or what He's created. That said, it shouldn't be restricted or committing a sin to voice my opinion about these politicians, who's trying to start another war. If only politicians started complaining about injustices the way the majority of Black people have complained for years. Then they will understand the crisis they've faced, trying to survive under their rules. Constantly, being blocked from the list. Having good housing, and equal opportunity. Americans are still waiting for our leaders to revise a new approach to help solve problems many of our Elders are experiencing without understanding their rules.

I suggest the only way we're get results is by striking, refusing to pay Taxes, until congress is willing to meet our demands legislatively. Black Americans have always acted too passive supplying them with their Tax money. However, if they stopped it will surely get their attention showing how desperate they are to end this problem!! While protecting business owners from losing their businesses by complying with their request to strike! Let it be known, if the government and the judicial system won't be responsible for the safety of Black people, let's consider that when we vote!!

Look it up, the constitution says no Taxation without (representation). It should be clear and it is they weren't represented through the years properly in areas of government and the judicial system that failed to protect them from being killed. Still, so far politicians won't pass a no hanging law in congress, just think about what that means to people who have a reputation of being (hung)? Hey if that doesn't get Black people attention, knowing it will be difficult for anyone to support them going soft on politicians refusing to help them. I think it's time to review seriously what these republicans are engaged in, if we want to save this Country from tyranny.

It's obvious, politicians have used another way to fight wars against Americans without using weapons. Furthermore, realizing their fighting technique to win is through the ballet box? Unfortunately, all our efforts will be wiped out completely, if we allow politicians to determined who's eligible to vote in different States. This isn't a joke listening to their strategy to win, makes me wonder what happened to the morals we teach our children growing up?! This is just the beginning of republican's methods of showing the American people they can't stand losing Elections?!

Please keep this in mind because it's true. My son Samuel C, said, "the reason politicians can obstruct people from voting, is because only White people have the right to vote." According to their laws Black people were given the privilege to vote through legislation, therefore politicians can change their laws whenever it's convenient." However, if that's true Black people should consider those options when they pay Taxes or volunteer to fight or die in their armed forces?! So, after they risk their lives overseas and come back to their families here in America, they should ask Congress are their families still living in poverty?

Ask politicians when they come back from winning wars, why are their families still asking for equal justice here under the law? If politicians say nothing has changed, then what other benefits are these soldiers fighting for, or intitle to aside of their military rank? Still, they're depending on the government to compensate them for a few extra dollars every month for being wounded in battle. In comparison to what white people receive, it's like lapping crumbs falling from a dog's master's table.

Unfortunately, the difference is politicians who sent them overseas are cruising around on Yachts and living in Mansions. Yet men and women who served in their armed forces are still the ones suffering from battle fatigue and anxiety and other problems. Yes, I must admit there are Americans young and old who volunteer their help when they protest, knowing war is inevitable. If we don't change our ideals politically, to serve those who serve us with their lives. I bet it will start a wave of violence and death between White and colorful people here and around the world.

For years, we've assumed associations brings on similarities in people and I believe it's true. Seriously, if people don't care if their prayers aren't answered concerning these issues. I don't see the logic in continuously praying for changes you're not receiving for your-self, or to help others? When I was a boy, my parents believed God may not come when you want Him, but He's right on time? However, it's unfortunate for her and others their prayers weren't answered during their life time or after their deaths. So why not ask somebody, what constitutes urgencies, if no one is responding to any of your life and death emergencies?

We should know some politicians are too cowardly to answer this question honestly? These facts about the way Palms treat Black people, they can't hide anymore. Americans know the answer, but politicians won't stop being a hypocrite and say it to their faces, if they're Americans or not? If you haven't noticed they're acting like this country only belong to them, because they're the majority in this Country. There are times when we ignore facts, forgetting White men control every aspect of our lives. Nevertheless, I hope Americans will wake up, and admit it's time for all of them to come to terms about what their statis is in this Country? Or stop believing you are an (American), when you're not treated like one!!

Tragically, all of us should know if Blacks were treated as Americans, Mr. Amir wouldn't have been assassinated trying to defend his-self. While police officers were invading his home shooting at him waking up being terrorized by gun fire! However, did those officers lose their jobs or go to prison for Murder killing the wrong person? (No)! Now it's politicians' chance to prove me wrong about the majority of them being killers, by giving their support celebrating (African Americans Day). Yes, it seems the more things change in America the more they stay the same. Maybe they should've taken a lesson from the Jews who don't celebrate the birthday of Hitler, who was responsible for Millions of them dying?

Further, it would seem logical to think on the other-side of this equation. Once some of their children become adults, it's only natural they would feel proud and motivated to follow the same legacy of their so-called heroic forefathers who owned slaves. I believe that's why these politicians are still fighting hard to keep their Confederate tradition (alive in the South). They do it flying the confederate flag in the faces of Black people to keep them reminded of their legacy. So, if slavery is the undying soul of America that won't be relinquished from the mind of some Americans, then war is inevitable. For those who's still fighting for the same concept slavery was based on. Wakeup guys, and act like this fight against them is urgent, and be honest about who's to blame for allowing these politicians to take us back in time? Remember when you hear some of them saying let's make America great again, they're not speaking to (all Americans)!

CHAPTER 14

Another Force for Justice

I guess these tragedies we're experiencing now could be another way of karma punishing all of us with the Corona-virus, and other deceases throughout the world. For allowing an unfit ex-president and other world leaders to participate in unlawful activities that helped caused the death of Millions of people. Obviously, now they're feeling more confident advocating his message of death throughout this Country, without fear of him or his political clan going to prison. You might've guessed at my age, I haven't seen real justice in this country except for Gorge Floyd, and a few others including Obama care. This is something Black people can be proud of mentioning it politically or judicially to their children. For years progress has been lacking helping some Americans survive. This injustice has continued since I was old enough to understand the difference between right and wrong.

Sure, I've considered myself an American, but right now I feel it doesn't matter, what really matters is the future of our children and grandchildren. I hope there will be a time, when Black people won't be restricted from acting in self-defense, and be Vindicated killing their attacker because they (feared for their lives)? Or, does a person who's wearing a police Uniforms life have more value than ordinary citizens that's paying their salaries? Now judges are saying they can't stop their defense lawyers from restricting Black people from serving as jurors when White people are accused of murdering them!

It's time to put an end to some of the procedures of the judicial system, refusing to penalize juror's for committing crimes not rendering guilty verdicts according to the evidence. Simply, because of technicalities in their laws that favors an acquittal, when the evidence proved otherwise. Then again, I wonder why Americans still believe White people are the only ones who's qualified intellectually to be in Congress? However, you would think after seeing the same faces, who's not qualified to serve Americans, they should be anxious to see a different look in attitude from the way it's been for hundreds of years?!

Also, it's time for all Americans to consider another problem that needs their attention. To investigate those individuals who've been incarcerated unjustly for years. It's time to stop these judges who's void of conscience using the name of God as a camouflage, to take advantage of people who's ignorant of their laws. If Americans would take the time to search their records it will prove there were cases that deceived them by using those words, in (God we trust). Only, to justify the horror they committed, by sentencing people to more years than the law required for the crime.

For years it was hard for Americans to accept some of those officers of the court Black and White Judges and Lawyers couldn't be trusted. It's no secret, how they neglected to perform their duties by Vindicating those Black prisoners who were innocent of the crimes they were accused of. Now I understand what those words in God we trust meant to those judges, which is absolutely nothing!! Just, in case you haven't notice, Millions of people generally don't seem to be worried about going to Heaven anymore! Obviously, if going to Heaven was a priority, these politicians would be more concerned about how they treat people's civil right issues.

Moreover, it shouldn't be hard to admit after so much suffering the republicans are showing how good they are deceiving people who voted for them. We should know some of these news reporters especially the ones on Fox news wouldn't be smiling making jokes and excuses if that racist mob were Black men and women trying to over-throw the Government. Nevertheless, we know if Black Americans displayed that kind of violence against any White man, or woman. There would be hundreds if not thousands of unarmed Black people lying in the streets dying or dead with news reports complimenting White officers, for their actions of heroism!

That said, now we've seen the difference in policing when it's not Black people involved. Which should also be an assault against every-body, knowing our fallen Veteran's died, sacrificing their lives for nothing. Just think about if we can't acknowledge the difference between patriots from traitors regardless of their skin color, then we're not worthy to be called Americans? I believe Palms are afraid darker skinned officials will eventually be the majority in congress, depending on who (Americans choose) to lead them in the future? I've listened to people bragging for years about this being the richest country in the world.

Nevertheless, you wouldn't be able to confirm it, once you've seen the dark alleys in East Baltimore, or in the cracked streets in Brooklyn N.Y. Those same sights of neglect are seen in many other sections of dilapidated buildings in poverty-stricken communities everywhere. Believe me I know how politicians ignored some people and their offspring's who've lived in those communities for generations. Just think about how difficult it is living under those conditions without politicians helping those Tax payers to live with dignity. If that's not considered neglect, of being unqualified to create laws making a healthier environment for everybody? Then their laws need (reparation) now!!

However, after experiencing sickness and death, you would think it would be easier for people to face facts, about the kind of politicians we've voted for? Nevertheless, Black people are still emerging from the bowels of our political system to gain recognition expressing their determination to fight for equality. If only some of these politicians could get a piece of the action, then they're understand what it means being poor in America. Living in broken homes without a mother or Father, also struggling every month to pay bills trying to survive living on a Welfare Check, that barely keeps them a float with a roof over their heads, and food to eat?

Still these people pay Taxes while the rich pay (nothing). Now we insist on a new system, after seeing politicians come to their communities walking around with a tough guy attitude with a crowd of armed-bodyguards. Surrounding them acting scared of being seen alone in the poorest communities. I guarantee, if they spent a few hours aside of their comfort zone, in one of those ghetto sections of Brownsville in Brooklyn N.Y. The next time you saw or heard from those politicians, they would have a plan within minutes to end racism. (Lol). Just because I'm using humor to get my point across, understand this is not a joke. I know those of you Black and White who have children and grandchildren, I'm sure you would like a better life for them, than what the older generation have experienced during their lifetime.

With all due respect if you're a follower of Mr. Donald Trump and his clan remember, our children and grandchildren won't tolerate being told to follow orders from anyone they can't trust? Also remember they're still waiting, but it's obvious republicans haven't acknowledge (Black lives matters). However, I guess for them it's no surprise because we haven't seen any legislation passed helping their cause against racism. If that's not a crime then nothing they're doing illegally protesting, burning buildings shouldn't be compared to the crimes we've seen committed at the Capital.

I know after a few months these actions of Piracy they've committed will no longer be televised or reported, just like the rest of their acts of violence. Next, we're probably be talking about more police shootings of Black people being killed again on their way home. Why, because they looked suspicious being unarmed, forcing White police officers to make more split-seconds decisions if they live or die?! Yeah, the foul smell about this issue is more than just disgraceful. Their actions are beyond being reasonable to believe these Cops are innocent of Murder.

I wonder, will it be necessary to go to war again for their voting rights to be restored, which is also part of their survival. Unfortunately, Americans haven't made it clear enough, there will be consequences for killing anyone for speaking or writing about Black history? Only, if Americans are ready now to be fair, acknowledging reporters aren't asking White people, the same questions about suffering in this Country. It seems there's no escape from this problem of racism because it's worldwide and controlled and acted out by some White men and women around the world. That's why they're fighting for justice to show the impact of what it means to be Black in America.

The truth is every country controlled by white people; it seems they've always had a problem with accepting different Ethnic groups as part of the Human race. Please don't forget how (Mr. Marcus Garvey) was treated in this Country years ago! Yet, some Black people who are oppressed continue to serve this Country with undying gratitude. However, sometimes, when I close my eyes at night, I know there's something going on that's foul. Which blocks me from feeling optimistic about how I feel about America's ideals of justice being a myth all of these years. Honestly when I think about Millions of Americans dying believing in false promises of hope, it should finally open our eyes and face reality, that we've been bamboozled.

There are no words to express how I feel right now writing this book about those 3 subjects mentioned in this book. It seems every attempt I make trying to discuss those subjects with the public, it seems to creates a lot of anger and fear! (Why)? It's because when I wake up, I realize this isn't a dream, what these republicans are doing under the leadership of Donald Trump, is worse than having a nightmare! Just knowing it could be the end of a mixed culture of Human-beings who could've been joined together, if we're willing to accept each other as human-being instead of slaves!!

CHAPTER 15

Be aware of self-destruction!

It's strikingly ironic to witness Americans fearing the forceful conquest of their nation by another country while overlooking the power struggles fueled by politicians' egos. These politicians perceive themselves as superior to people of other ethnic groups, which, in turn, influences some Americans to attack the very heart of democracy, the Capitol, based on false beliefs. It's a painful legacy to pass down to the next generation—a legacy that dismantles and defeats the most powerful country in the world due to hatred towards Black people, who are rightful citizens of this land.

History, with its undeniable facts, will also bear witness to how this same kind of hatred has destroyed nations throughout time, including the appalling mistreatment of Jews by the Germans. Discrimination, fueled by hatred, has repeatedly proven to be the downfall of societies. It is essential that we learn from these dark chapters of history and work towards a future where unity and respect prevail over division and prejudice. It is important to acknowledge the historical accounts that demonstrate how hate has defeated powerful figures like Pharaoh, the king of Egypt, and his army. Historians have documented the downfall of Pharaoh due to the same reasons that perpetuated slavery. This serves as a crucial lesson that our leaders seem to lack the foresight to address this problem without costing the lives of millions of Americans in the process. Engaging in methods that inflict death only perpetuates a mentality that we cannot survive with.

Unfortunately, we find ourselves deeply divided, following the same destructive patterns that have destroyed other nations. Moreover, amidst this turmoil, we are confronted with the ongoing battle against the coronavirus. We, as darker-skinned individuals, face a higher vulnerability to the virus, as our skin color seems to trigger racial hatred that leads to acts of violence against us. My research reveals that this infection does not pose the same level of threat to the general public; its focus appears to be primarily aimed at killing darker-skinned Americans and others around the world who share a similar skin texture. Personally, I find it disheartening that this seems to be the only infection in medical history or science that specifically targets one particular group the darker-skinned individuals.

Whether one chooses to believe this or not, it is deeply frustrating for me to discuss these issues as they often stir up controversy. Nonetheless, it is crucial that we confront these difficult truths and work towards creating a society that is free from such biases and discriminatory practices.

I must acknowledge that discussing these issues can be disheartening, knowing that only a few Americans are willing to engage in open conversation or take the time to educate themselves about these pressing matters. However, I hold onto hope that through reading this book, individuals will become aware of the degrading issues that continue to fuel wars and conflicts. I hope it sparks a difference in the way they perceive and respond to Black people, both now and in the future. It is my sincere belief that if people embrace the teachings within this book, it can forge an unbreakable chain of solidarity, particularly among those who seek to eradicate this deadly cancer of racism. I write about these hot-button issues because I know there are Americans who are hungry for the raw truth, who yearn to understand why some individuals harbor such deep-seated anger and animosity towards Black people. Only time will tell if I have successfully reached the hearts and minds of men and women, encouraging them to confront the uncomfortable truths that they may have previously avoided. Yet, I implore us all to recognize that racism has a destructive reputation, capable of permanently shattering lives if we do not challenge and overcome this poisonous way of thinking. This sickness permeates like a fungus, infiltrating the minds of those who falsely claim superiority over their fellow human beings.

We must be wise enough to understand that true character is not determined by the color of our skin, but by the moral principles we uphold without compromise. Let us strive to create a society where the preservation and respect for all human life are central to our beliefs.

I firmly believe that taking a giant leap towards humility is a significant step towards fulfilling our purpose in life. It is through embracing humility that we can differentiate ourselves as individuals. I believe it would be beneficial if some Americans approached their pastors or ministers and asked them whether one can claim to be a Christian while aligning politically with Mr. Donald Trump. If the answer is yes, it is important to inquire about what the Bible says regarding liars. It is crucial that if we truly believe in Jesus, we must align our actions with the teachings of the Bible without making excuses once we have vowed to obey its principles. It is essential to understand that we cannot create our own methods of serving Jesus if we genuinely desire to live a Christian life. Any deviation from the teachings of the Bible would categorize us as hypocrites or sinners among Christians. When choosing to follow the teachings of Jesus, it is crucial to embody ethics and a deep sense of pride in our own humanity and that of others. This stands in stark contrast to following the path of Mr. Trump. His leadership has proven detrimental to Americans due to his demands of unquestioning obedience in his quest for world domination. Indeed, if we pay close attention to his actions, it becomes evident how his followers are fearful of speaking the truth, as it appears to be forbidden unless it aligns with his approval. Moreover, agreeing to his rules requires suppressing the inclination to act morally and stifling our conscience, which urges us to do what is right according to the Constitution and towards our fellow human beings. Instead, we should be teaching our children at home and in our schools to be individuals who exemplify integrity and refuse to be influenced by accepting bribes that may cause harm or even death to others.

It is disheartening to witness that sometimes the mentors we look up to do not practice what they preach, particularly when it comes to honesty. Throughout my youth, my family and I engaged in discussions about religion and its transformative power, believing that accepting Jesus and living in accordance with the teachings of the Bible would grant us eternal life after death. While I have refrained from criticizing others' religious beliefs, I have questioned the lifestyles of those who claim to be Christians but do not align their actions with the principles they profess. Reflecting on my own journey, there was a time when my entire family, including my parents, siblings, and myself, were known as Christians. I was involved in singing and preaching, prioritizing my beliefs over the reality of my circumstances. In my family, we had missionaries, including my mother, and the legacy of their faith in Jesus has been passed down through generations, with some of my children, particularly my firstborn, Ms. Jervel Gilbert, obtaining degrees in Theology. However, my daughter Sylva has developed her own unique perspective on life. Throughout the years, I have been fortunate to witness the blessings of seeing my great-grandchildren and even my great-great-grandchildren, which fills me with gratitude.

I can confidently say that I possess a deep understanding of Christianity and what it means to be a follower of Jesus. Growing up, like many other families, we engaged in conversations about various topics, but politics rarely entered our discussions. Our primary focus revolved around the life of Jesus and his disciples, as that was our central interest at the time. However, as I have journeyed through life and faced its harsh realities, my perspectives have evolved. I have become more acutely aware of life and death situations, particularly the unjust killings of Black people in America. This awareness has prompted me to make a conscious decision to dedicate myself to serving and contributing to the eradication of racism, an infection that has claimed the lives of countless individuals.

I hope that my choice to write about this pervasive problem is something that would make my ancestors and the soldiers who fought in the Civil War proud. They endured immense hardships, fighting for their lives, unaware that this racial war would persist even in the 21st century. Through this book, I aim to shed light on the deep-seated prejudices and animosity some individuals harbor towards African Americans. It is a tribute to their unwavering struggle during tumultuous times, fighting for a cause that was undeniably worth the battle.

I am honored to remind Americans of the limited choices our ancestors faced: to either remain enslaved or to fight for freedom. It is because of their courageous decisions and tireless labor that many of their descendants and others now reap the benefits. Their sacrifices laid the foundation for the progress we have achieved, and it is our responsibility to honor their legacy by continuing the fight for equality and justice. I am well aware of the immense pride our community takes in joining the armed forces and sacrificing their lives to fight for equality in other countries. While we acknowledge that America is far from perfect, it provides a level of protection through firearms that others may never have experienced. Initially, I didn't realize how emotionally draining it would be to write about the horror and grief our people have suffered, particularly when White individuals can make life or death decisions without any legitimate authority over Black lives. Let me clarify that while it is a serious matter to delve into these tragedies, my intention is not to incite conflict between racial groups. My true purpose is to shed more light on the experiences of those who should never have had to face death simply because they look different. This book aims to expose the raw truth from the perspective of an elderly Black man, allowing the world to accept or reject the harsh realities they have been eagerly awaiting. In the current state of affairs, numerous politicians disseminate lies that have a detrimental impact on the minds of millions of young people, affecting their well-being both now and potentially in the future. It is crucial to remember that the kind of global exposure and awareness we have today regarding the cruel treatment inflicted upon these individuals was not present for centuries. Despite the confusion our ancestors may have had about where a better world existed, I have no doubt that they knew it was on the horizon. While some may look to space, I prefer to believe that a better world can be found right here on Earth.

I reflect on the place that God created for the human race to exist: Earth. According to what's written in the Bible, some Christians believe they will sing praises to God for eternity when they are raised from the dead. However, I must admit that the belief in an afterlife is rooted in tradition and faith, rather than concrete facts. We should recognize the distinction between what we believe and what we can truly know. Furthermore, it is essential to understand that every individual has the right to hold their own beliefs or disbeliefs, even if they differ from our own. These differences in belief should not hinder the love we have for our family or fellow human beings. In seeking truth, it is crucial to assess the realistic facts and determine whether the concepts presented are worthy of consideration, regardless of whether they are from the Bible or any other book. Now, we should pause and consider if we approach spiritual doctrines, such as the Jewish teachings, with an open mind and critically evaluate the credibility of their authors. It is important for both Jews and Gentiles to take these words of truth seriously, as it can make a significant difference in their lives. We need to impart this understanding to the next generation, helping them differentiate between hyperbole and reality regarding life and death.

Let us move forward together, acknowledging that the idea of a mystical world like Heaven physically existing somewhere in space is a belief held by believers. However, it is important to recognize that Heaven may exist as a concept within the minds of those who believe, rather than as a tangible place. It is crucial to accept logical explanations from those who discern the difference between facts and fiction.

In conclusion, I have come to realize the dangers of being misled and blinded by misinformation regarding the location and nature of Heaven. I now strive to convince others to embrace the understanding that Heaven, as a physical realm, is a fantasy. Instead, it exists within the minds of believers who may choose to reject logical explanations. May we all seek the truth and discern between fact and fiction. The End.

Milton Keynes UK
Ingram Content Group UK Ltd.
UKHW040716201123
432908UK00002B/422